BY
DIVINE
DESIGN

To Margaret,

Romans 8:28,29

Dave Rey

BY DIVINE DESIGN

A Devotional Tour With

Dana Key

BROADMAN & HOLMAN PUBLISHERS

Nashville, Tennessee

4240-15
0-8054-4015-1

Dewey Decimal Classification: 242.63
Subject Heading: Youth—Religious Life\Daily Devotions
Library of Congress Card Catalog Number: 95-31590

Published in association with the literary agency of Alive Communications, Inc., 1465 Kelly Johnson Blvd., Suite 320, Colorado Springs, CO 80902

Unless otherwise noted, Scripture quotations are from the Holy Bible, New International Version, © 1973, 1978, 1984 by the International Bible Society.

Library of Congress Cataloging-in-Publication Data
Key, Dana.
    By divine design / Dana Key
      p. cm.
    ISBN 0-8054-4015-1
    1. Youth—Prayer-books and devotions—English.
  2. Devotional calendars. I. Title.
    BV4531.2.K46 1995
    242'.63—dc20

                        95-31590
                        CIP

99 98 97 96 95 5 4 3 2 1

To the love of my life, Anita.

CONTENTS

A Personal Word

THIS BOOK IS A devotional and Bible study book that has been prayerfully created to help you understand your place in God's great plan. Each devotional was written to help you learn the biblical principles for discovering and doing God's will. They take about ten minutes to read and five minutes to complete the feature called "Just Do It." (Some Just Do Its will require more time.) You will find that all of the material falls into one of three categories: Sovereignty, Scripture, or Service.

Sovereignty because knowing the immensity of God and the completeness of His plan builds confidence and strengthens faith. Scripture because it illuminates the path that the Christian should take. Service because it is in doing His will that we ultimately achieve our greatest fulfillment.

You'll regularly need a Bible, a pen or pencil, note cards, and/or a notepad to complete the Just Do It segments. You'll be tempted to skip these, but let me beg you not to. The Just Do It portions are there to help you be "a doer of the word" not just "a hearer." If you skip them you'll miss half the blessings that await you.

I suggest you keep this book and your supplies together so you won't have to search for anything after completing the reading segments. It's also a good idea to find a consistent place and time each day to complete your reading and prayer. If that means getting up twenty minutes earlier, take the challenge. It will be worth it to you.

May Jesus meet you each day and empower you to *know* and *do* His will.

YOUR BROTHER,
DANA

1
No Fear

And anyone who does not carry his cross and follow me cannot be my disciple.

LUKE 14:27

DON WAS A GREEN BERET IN VIETNAM. He still wore his beret everywhere, and rumor had it that he kept a machine gun in his car. He was obviously proud to be recognized as a former member of America's elite fighting force. In Vietnam this division of the armed forces served with distinction. Specially trained to take on only the most perilous missions, the Green Berets spent much of their time well behind enemy lines, deep inside of Cambodia and North Vietnam.

After the war, Don resumed his career as a songwriter and musician. Consequently, I would often run into him at the recording studio. Most times it was late at night. Like the vast majority of musicians, Don operated on MST (Musician Standard Time).

One evening, just before midnight, I noticed a crowd gathering around the studio coffeepot. Don was talking, and everyone was listening. That meant we civilians were in for a treat. Don was a paralyzing storyteller, and this one turned out to be his best.

Don had a reputation for being the baddest guy around, so we were surprised when he launched into the details of his fear of battle. He spoke of nightmares, cold sweats, and even nausea. But what took us all off guard was what amounted to a confession of his embarrassment at being shown up day after day by a group of specially selected South Koreans.

According to Don, they were the bravest fighting force he had ever seen. Though small in stature, they fought relentlessly. Never retreating. Always advancing. They stayed to themselves, saying little. Each of them wore a prominent black armband.

Don said it took some time, but eventually he got to know one of the South Koreans well enough to ask about the armbands. The Korean responded, "The armband means I've come to die." You see, each of these guys had lost loved ones and possessions to the advance of communism fifteen years earlier in Korea. Each of them, by putting on the armband was saying, "I don't intend to go home from this one. I've come to Vietnam to die."

As I listened to this story, it occurred to me that this was the reason for their heroism. When a man makes the decision that he has come to die, he has put to rest the nagging questions that drain the valor of the strongest men. If dying is your ambition, then death brings only delight. When you have come to die, no enemy can harm you; nothing you desire can be taken away from you. Dead men have no possessions.

Jesus asks you and me to settle that supreme issue as we come to Him. "If anyone would come after me, he must deny himself and take up his cross daily and follow me" (Luke 9:23).

It has been forgotten that the cross is the executioner's tool. Today the crucifix is a piece of jewelry, and unfortunately familiarity breeds indifference. We need to view the cross as if it were an ancient electric chair or a firing squad. Then we would be constantly reminded that the cross represents a call to the death of self. Perhaps then we would be able to serve Christ with the courage of a man who has nothing to lose, including his life. In losing all, we would surely gain the courage to live for Christ with no fear.

JUST DO IT

FIND OUT if your church or another church in your area provides meals for the homeless. Volunteer to help. Participate in any street-level, low-glamour ministry this year that will allow you to rub shoulders with some of the selfless superstar servants of Christ, those who invisibly go about the work of building the kingdom.

> *Do not let this Book of the Law depart from your mouth; meditate on it day and night, so that you may be careful to do everything written in it. Then you will be prosperous and successful.*
>
> JOSHUA 1:8

2
The Lighthouse

He calls his own sheep by name and leads them out. . . . He goes on ahead of them, and his sheep follow.

JOHN 10:3–4

TWO LIGHTS BLINKED IN THE FOG just off the Carolina coast. One flashed, "Veer to port four degrees. Our ship has the right of way." The other blinked, "Turn starboard four degrees immediately. You do not have the right of way." The first operator fired back, "Yield the right of way. I am a captain." The other blinked in response, "Turn four degrees starboard. I am a seaman second class." The captain furiously flashed back, "Turn four degrees to port. I am a battleship." The light in the night responded, "Turn starboard four degrees now. I am a lighthouse."

There are some arguments in life that you just can't win. You can argue all you want, but you are headed for the rocks. This is what it's like to argue with God's Word. I knew a girl who said in response to a verse of Scripture, "Well, if that's the way God is, then I'm just not going to believe in Him." Who loses that battle? You can either believe God's Word or crash on the rocks.

There are times when the Bible teaches us things that human reason says is a contradiction. We find rest under a yoke (see Matthew 11:28–30). We reign by serving (see Mark 10:42–44). We become wise by becoming fools for Christ (see 1 Corinthians 1:20–21). We are made free by becoming bond servants (see Romans 6:10). We are brought to life by dying (see John 12:24–25).

The Bible gives us instructions that seem foolish to the world because they are not supported by common sense or logic. It tells us to pray to an invisible God. To listen for His inaudible voice. To feel unexplainable peace. It asks us to believe in miracles that transcend the unbelievable. These are the kinds of things that often cause the unbeliever to crash upon the rocks.

The Book of Judges in the Old Testament tells about a dark time for Israel. The people of Israel repeatedly turned from God and did what was right in their own eyes. Samson was such a man, filled with strength and passion, yet both led him into the most grievous sins of the flesh. He disregarded God's instructions to the people of Israel and was betrayed by his Philistine lover, Delilah. He followed his heart, and it led him to his death.

God's people wandered into the worship of false gods. The Lord often punished their sin by sending neighboring powers against them, but the people of Israel continued to do what they saw fit. They were sincerely doing what they felt was right, but not what was right according to God's Word. They did what was "right in their own eyes," lending weight to the notion that it's possible to be sincere and still be sincerely wrong.

The age in which we live is comparable to the period of the judges. Sincere Christians are misguided concerning the social issues of our day. Some have preferred their own opinions rather than Scripture, causing them to spout the most absurd stupidity. For example, sincere Christians can be overheard saying things like, "It's better for birth to be terminated by abortion than to be born into poverty or an unwanted situation," or "Sex outside of marriage is only wrong when there is an absence of love and commitment." These may sound like the very noble platitudes of an enlightened society, but they are, in fact, stumbling blocks on the dark path of fallen human reason.

Sometimes our senses fail us. If we follow them alone, they will surely lead us to our deaths. One of the highest hurdles a new pilot must face is that of learning to fly on instruments alone. There are times in fog and rain where life or death depends on trusting your instruments to bring you in safely. A phenomena called spatial distortion can sometimes make a pilot feel that the information he is receiving from these instruments is wrong. Up feels like down; down feels like up. There are many examples of pilots who have crashed because they were unable to put aside their feelings and trust their instruments.

Those feelings are understandable. It is possible that one of those electronic gadgets could give bad advice. That is why almost every navigation system on an aircraft is redundant. Commercial airliners have three altitude gauges. If one disagrees with the others, you can bet it is unreliable.

The natural man is born with a moral compass called conscience, but it has been severely damaged by sin and very often gives us unreliable information. Still, God has given us all we need to avoid a crash landing. He has given us more than just one moral compass. He has given us a complete instrument panel. He has given us the sixty-six books found in His Word. Each of them harmonizes with the moral guidance given to us by each of the others. The information is reliable, and when we find ourselves in a moral fog we can trust that God's Word is true no matter what we may feel. Each promise can be relied upon. Each principle will lead us safely from danger because it is true.

The choice is simple. You can either heed the instructions given you from the lighthouse of God's Word or you can follow logic, common sense, or popular opinion onto the jagged rocks of unbelief.

JUST DO IT

WRITE THIS verse on a note card. Carry it with you and memorize it.

Do not let this Book of the Law depart from your mouth; meditate on it day and night, so that you may be careful to do everything written in it. Then you will be prosperous and successful.

JOSHUA 1:8

3
Love God, Hate Sin

Continue to work out your salvation with fear and trembling, for it is God who works in you to will and to act according to his good purpose.

PHILIPPIANS 2:12–13

I HAD A FRIEND WHO HAD JUST finished a year of reading through the Bible. Jokingly I asked him, "What did it say?" My friend replied, "I'm God and you're not." That says it all. I love those little get-to-the-point sayings. Christian recording artist Mylon Lefevre has one that describes the Christian life, "Love God, hate sin." That about sums up all that God expects of us: love Him and hate evil. It's easy to say but hard to do.

Love is a wornout, abused word today. In popular music and literature, love is either something you make, which is a synonym for sex, or it is something you fall into, which means warm, fuzzy feelings. When the Bible tells us in the greatest of the commandments to "Love the Lord your God, with all your heart, soul and mind," it has neither of these meanings in view. Real love for God has little to do with fuzzy feelings and nothing to do with sex.

Love is a conscious choice that is demonstrated by outward obedience. Jesus said to His disciples, "If you love me, you will obey what I command" (John 14:15). The only sure way our love can be demonstrated is by our adherence to Christ's commands. Feelings come and go with the winds of circumstances. They can even be counterfeited by Satan. Thus, they are unreliable indicators of the depth of your relationship to Christ. Obedience is the true test of loving Jesus.

Consider what Jesus will say before the great throne of judgment. "Then the King will say to those on his right, 'Come, you who are blessed by my Father; take your inheritance, the kingdom prepared for you since the creation of the world. For I was hungry and you gave me something to eat, I was thirsty and you gave me something to drink, I was a stranger and you invited me in, I needed clothes and you clothed me, I was sick and you looked after me, I was in prison and you came to visit me. . . . I tell you the truth, whatever you did for one of the least of these brothers of mine, you did for me'" (Matthew 25:34–36, 40).

No one is asked to step forward to give a testimony. Time for talk has passed. When the sheep and the goats are separated, it is not on the basis of their words but rather on the basis of their deeds. Love for Christ is more eloquently spoken by tiny deeds of kindness. That's what it means to love God. But what about hating sin?

If we are completely honest, we must admit that in our Christian experience there are times when we love God and hate sin, and others when we like God and love sin. Sometimes we share God's utter repugnance toward sin, but other times we are dazzled by its attraction. We leave our sin behind with the same enthusiasm as Lot's wife showed in leaving Sodom—reluctantly looking back over our shoulders.

My two-year-old nephew, Ryan, was in desperate need of a diaper change. The evidence filled the air. When my sister, Jaime, asked him if he needed a new diaper, Ryan, with convincing sincerity, said, "No." Jaime warned, "Son, don't lie to me." He responded, "I want to lie."

God knows that we sin because we sometimes listen to our old sin nature, and that nature "wants to." It's unbelievable, but that's why He gives us a new nature and changes our "want to." Philippians 2:13 says, "for it is God who works in you to will and to act according to his good purpose." God is at work causing us to will what is right and hate what is wrong. What a miserable life Christians would have if we were forced to live righteously while eternally longing to sin. Heaven would be hell if we were captive there in body while our hearts longed for Sodom.

God is changing our very natures. Through the ongoing process of sanctification, He is preparing us to be citizens of heaven. He is creating in our hearts the love of holiness and the hatred for sin. Not only does it ensure that we will get to heaven, it means that we will love being there.

JUST DO IT

TAKE A FEW minutes to prayerfully confess those sins you love most. Think about the agony Jesus suffered to purchase your forgiveness for that sin. Then ask God to change your "want to."

4
THE PRISONER OF CHILLON

*"This is the one I esteem: he who is humble and
contrite in spirit, and trembles at my word."*

ISAIAH 66:2

*I would gladly sacrifice my all to the Son
and here I'll gladly serve him as
the prisoner of Chillon*

IN THE 1500S A MOVEMENT SPRANG UP that held that the Bible was
a higher moral authority than the pope. Those who believed this
found themselves in direct opposition to the Roman Catholic
Church. One of the most haunting stories of this epic involves a
little-known monk who sought no publicity.

Legend has it that a humble priest named François
Bonnivard had a little disagreement with the count of Savoy, a
dignitary of Montreux, Switzerland. It seems that Bonnivard was
one of those daring reformers who believed that even the pope
should submit to the authority of God's written Word. The monk,
a humble prelate of a local monastery, had no power to prevent
his being imprisoned in the dungeon under the castle of Chillon
(pronounced she-own). Seven hundred feet above Lake Geneva,
the prisoner of Chillon was chained to a stone column with just
enough slack to look out a window and see the snow-covered
mountains in the distance, but he could not see the lake below.

Years later, as a guest at the Chillon castle, Lord Byron wrote
one of the most haunting poems in literary history called "The
Prisoner of Chillon." It described the lonely day-to-day struggle

Bonnivard fought to keep his commitment to the authority of God's Word as well as his own sanity. The monk, with chained ankles and a bed of stones, never recanted. This kind of saint belongs in the Hebrews 11 "Faith Hall of Fame"—a man of deep convictions and the courage to sacrifice all for them.

I toured Savoy's castle while in Europe in 1991, almost five hundred years after the prisoner of Chillon had carved grooves into the floor by dragging his chains relentlessly across those stones. Struggling to appear interested in the tour, I walked from room to endless room. Truthfully, I had come to see the final room on the tour—the dungeon.

When that moment arrived, I looked through the stone window and saw the snow-covered mountains that must have looked much the same five hundred years ago to Bonnivard. I saw the iron ring that held his chain to the stones. And just above and to the right, I saw the chiseled name of Lord Byron, protected from tourists by a piece of clear plastic. Then, to my astonishment, just below that, I saw my own name.

I was startled to see my name carved into that column. My name isn't Bob Smith; it's not that common. In fact, I've never seen my name written on the pages of a phone book or a bathroom wall. Dana Key is just not a name you hear every day. But there it was, deeply carved into that gray, tarnished stone next to Lord Byron's name. I stared for a long time before I said anything to my companions, wanting to make sure I wasn't dreaming. When I looked over and saw the expressions on their faces, I realized they had seen it, too.

My friends know I could not easily be mistaken for a mystic. If anything, the opposite is true. But this was too weird, especially in the light of what had been taking place in my life at home. You see, just before leaving for Europe, after months of wrestling, I had told my wife, Anita, that I had learned that the Lord wanted me to have a single ministry focus for the rest of my life: defending and promoting His Word.

For Bonnivard, standing up for God's Word came with a price. Deep down he must have longed to tell the count of Savoy, "I was mistaken," and then walk the few short miles back to his home. Yet his walks were in three-foot circles. He dragged his tear-stained chains across those cold stones day after day. Still, Bonnivard was faithful. I'm only guessing, but I'll bet that he was clinging to what I call a lifetime verse. These are the ones that you hang on to in tough times. As long as I'm guessing, I'll say it was this one: "This is the one I esteem: he who is humble and contrite in spirit, and trembles at my word" (Isaiah 66:2).

JUST DO IT

MEMORIZE ONE of the following Scriptures:

How can a young man keep his way pure? By living according to your word.

PSALM 119:9

Do not let this Book of the Law depart from your mouth; meditate on it day and night, so that you may be careful to do everything written in it. Then you will be prosperous and successful.

JOSHUA 1:8

Blessed is the man who does not walk in the counsel of the wicked or stand in the way of sinners or sit in the seat of mockers. But his delight is in the law of the LORD, and on his law he meditates day and night. He is like a tree planted by streams of water, which yields its fruit in season and whose leaf does not wither. Whatever he does prospers.

PSALM 1:1–3

I use a technique I call "Hooking on to a Habit" to help me remember to read God's Word or spend time talking and listening to Him. Here's how it works. I love to read the sports page first thing in the morning. So I've hooked on to that habit by deciding to read the Bible *before* I read the sports page. This week, pick something you do *every* day and let that be your signal to read the Bible and pray. Remember, it takes three weeks to form a new habit.

5
Faith of a Child

"I tell you the truth, anyone who will not receive the kingdom of God like a little child will never enter it."

LUKE 18:17

"Is anything too hard for the LORD?"

GENESIS 18:14

THEY BUILT A RAUNCHY NIGHTSPOT right next door to Saint Lukewarm Baptist Church of God in Christ. The good folks of SLBCOGIC decided to start a prayer vigil. Amazingly, the nightclub's business dwindled so much they had to close the doors. This wasn't altogether good news, you see; the owner of the nightclub brought a lawsuit against the members of SLBCOGIC, accusing them of ruining his business with their prayers. The attorneys for the church argued there was no way their prayers could have had any effect on the poor performance of the club. The judge agreed. He ruled in favor of Saint Lukewarm, saying, "while the nightclub owner strongly believes in the power of prayer, the church membership does not."

Several years ago, I determined that it was time to teach my children how to pray. I am a big believer in keeping a prayer book so that you cannot only *remember* what you need to pray about, you have a *record* of when and how God answers your prayers.

I bought my kids a notebook and explained the procedure to them and also some of the ways God had blessed me through this approach. We talked about faith and God's ability to do anything.

We talked about how God loved to hear our prayers and promised to answer every one as He saw best.

While I was still talking, my wife was called to the phone, but I continued my sermonette. When Anita returned, she looked upset. There had been a car accident and a five-year-old girl named Kelly was in a coma. The doctors said that the chance of her survival was probably zero.

I could see it coming, and I have to admit I was a bit nervous. It was time to ask my kids to write down their first prayer request. I had so much wanted them to start with something easy. I didn't want God to look bad, and I sure didn't want them to have to cross out their first entry the next day.

Just as I feared, my son, Andrew, piped up and said, "Let's pray for Kelly." We did. We prayed for her for a week, and then Kelly opened her eyes and came out her coma. But the story doesn't stop here. The astonished doctors said that Kelly would live but she would never be able to talk. The kids continued to pray, and a few weeks later Kelly was talking. The doctors then said that Kelly would never be able to walk. But in a matter-of-fact way, my kids continued to believe God. Today, Kelly is not only walking, she is running.

The faith of children is so pure and so powerful. They haven't been taught to trust the word of doctors more than that of God. The world hasn't convinced them that there are some things God can't do. They simply believe that all things are possible when they are handed over to their heavenly Father.

Sometimes we say we believe in prayer, but our actions call us liars. If I say, "I believe in the power of prayer" but can't seem to find time for it, that clearly demonstrates I don't see a lot of value in it. If the church believed in the power of prayer there would likely be more praying and less preaching.

Jim Elliot once said, "God is still on His throne and a man is still on his footstool. There's only a knee's distance in-between." That distance was a Grand Canyon of doubt for me, but it was no distance at all for the tiny knees of my children. I set out to teach my children how to pray in faith; in the end it was my children who taught me.

Go ahead and ask God for the hard stuff. He can take care of Himself.

JUST DO IT

PURCHASE A small notebook and write down your prayer requests. Make a column for requests and another for the date of the Lord's answers. Leave plenty of room for words of praise and thanksgiving. You will need it.

6

PROMISES, PROMISES

This is the confidence we have in approaching God: that if we ask anything according to his will, he hears us.

1 JOHN 5:14

STEVE GREW UP IN A PRETTY TYPICAL Baptist home. He believed in miracles but was a tad bit skeptical about the whole faith-healing movement. Not that Steve or Baptists believe God is out of the healing business these days. It's just that they tend to be a little skittish about endorsing some of today's healers and "heal-ees." Like me, Steve wishes he could take people at face value who claim to be healers, but let's admit it, some of them have burned us in the past.

Before I go any further with this story, you need to know that Steve is just this side of being as blind as a bat. He is nearsighted with 20/275 vision. So when Steve saw Benny Hinn healing people that night on television, it really sparked his interest. Benny turned his attention from his studio guests to those watching at home and said, "If you wish to be healed, reach out toward your television." Steve's struggle with his eyesight was a real thorn in his flesh, and Benny was compelling. So Steve reached up to the television and prayed in faith, "God please heal my eyes."

Praying again into his pillow that night, Steve was making a deal with God when sleep interrupted him. As bright sunlight peaked through his window the next morning, he woke with the curiosity of a kid at Christmas. His eyes popped open wide and he focused on the ceiling (yes, really focused!).

"It's a miracle!" Steve cried out. He could actually see cracks in the ceiling plaster.

Launching from his undersized double bed, he skidded in his socks to the phone. You see, Steve remembered clearly the deal he offered God the night before: "God, if You see Your way clear to heal me, I promise I'll tell the whole world." God apparently had taken him up on the deal, and Steve was going to keep his part of the bargain. Trying to decide who to call first, he reached for the phone and began to dial. Then, like a truck, it hit him. He had fallen asleep with his contact lenses in. And standing there with the phone in his hand, Steve laughed out loud at himself, feeling both silly and dejected. Most of us who aren't walking on water yet are familiar with that feeling.

In 1985, we were told that Geneva's cancer had returned. Geneva was the kind of mother-in-law that nobody ever warned me about. She treated me like a son, not that I'm so lovable. She opened her heart to everyone whom God brought into her life. With a mother's love, she made me feel better about the world. It just didn't seem right for our "June Cleaver" to have cancer.

I prayed more than I had ever prayed before, yet day after day we watched Geneva slowly slip away. We had friends come in to help out. We sang. We prayed. We anointed her with oil. I called every superstar Christian I knew for advice. We exchanged words of encouragement with each other and Geneva. I found a promise in the Bible that I thought was given to us for Geneva's healing, and we rejoiced. Then Geneva died.

I spent the next few months wondering why my faith had failed. Wasn't God required to cooperate with faith as tiny as a mustard seed? I had named it and claimed it exactly as I had been told, but apparently no one had explained the rules to God. It was a painful way to discover that God won't be blackmailed by rules He didn't make. He is bound to His word, but not to promises that He never made.

Faith is not about conjuring up belief that God has promised you this or that; it's about trusting that if God promised, He will do it. "This is the confidence we have in approaching God: that if we ask anything according to his will, he hears us" (1 John 5:14).

Thus a life of faith begins by learning what God has already committed to us in the Bible as well as sharpening our spiritual ears so that we can better hear His voice.

Miracles still await those who are looking for what God wishes to do. Frustration, dejection, and silence lie ahead for those who think that God sits on His throne awaiting their instructions. Twisting God's arm to do your will is futile. In the end, it doesn't matter how badly you want a miracle or even need a miracle. Without His promise, what you're likely to get is a tap on the shoulder from reality whispering, "You're still just wearing your contact lenses."

JUST DO IT

SPEND YOUR prayer time asking Jesus to help you put your will aside. Tell Him you trust that He knows best what you need. Ask Him to help you see where He is going, so that you can follow Him more closely.

7
SATAN'S "I" PROBLEM

"He must become greater; I must become less."
JOHN 3:30

IN COLONIAL AMERICA, THERE WERE TWO basic tests for finding those in league with the devil. Neither one was a barrel of laughs, especially if you were the one being tested. A pin test went like this: Testers would take a sewing needle and prick the suspected witch all over. If a place was found on the person's skin where he felt no pain, this was considered evidence of Satanism. The numb spot was believed to have been left behind as the result of Satan's physical touch.

The second test (my personal favorite) was a real no-win situation. There were a variety of creative versions, but the basic test went something like this: Tie the suspect up and throw her into some water. If she floated, she was a witch. If she sank (and drowned), she was innocent. There's not much consolation in passing this test. If you floated, they'd quickly dry you off and burn you at the stake! If you drowned, you're name was cleared, but so what?

Today some of those in league with the devil are easy to spot. They wear 666 tattoos, pentagrams, and sport black hoods. They are shadowy figures who just have "Devil Worshiper" written all over them. But the more hideous and destructive of Satan's minions look pretty normal; in fact, they may even be seductively beautiful. After all, Satan has the ability to transform himself into an "angel of light" (2 Corinthians 11:14).

If appearance doesn't give a Satanist away, one thing always will: an undisguisable philosophy of life that focuses on self. In the tradition of their father, the sons of Satan inherit an "I" problem that can be easily seen by all.

Some Bible scholars think that Isaiah 14 is the account of Satan's downfall. Identified as the "morning star" that "fell from heaven," his way of life is made clear to us in five blasphemous boasts. "I will" is the disease, and what follows are the symptoms:

1. "I will ascend to heaven" (verse 13). James 4:15 tells us to say, "if it is the Lord's will" I will go here or do that. But Lucifer claims his right to go where he wishes. One of the most important credos of the Satan worshiper is, "I am free to do and go where I want." Christ's servants are bound to God's will.

2. "I will raise my throne above the stars of God" (verse 13). The stars of God refers to God's angelic servants. Satan claims the right to rule them. His followers take pride in how many people they lord over; the followers of Christ are concerned with how many people they are lifting up from beneath.

3. "I will sit enthroned on the mount of assembly, on the utmost heights of the sacred mountain" (verse 13). Satan desires to sit where the angels come to worship God. Not only does he desire to rule, he desires to be worshiped. Furthermore, he feels no guilt at being worshiped on the sacred mountain. As C. S. Lewis said, "The moderately evil man knows he is wicked but the truly evil man thinks himself O.K."

4. "I will ascend above the tops of the clouds" (verse 14). The clouds are a status symbol that proclaim you are as high as you can get. Selfish ambition to be number one burns continually in the heart of Satan and his followers. The status symbols that demonstrate their achievements dominate them.

5. "I will make myself like the Most High" (verse 14). The Most High is God, and Satan's ultimate ambition is to be like Him, but not in His holiness, love, or self-sacrificing compassion. He desires to be totally free, to rule others, to be worshiped, to be admired for his achievements, but never to love. These are the five glaring symptoms that follow the worst kind of "I" problem.

The most obvious trait of Satanism is selfishness. I was once asked to give an interviewer an example of Satanic music. To his surprise, I told him the most satanic song I'd ever heard was Paul Anka's "My Way."

What makes this song stand out in wickedness above others is that it has Satan's fingerprints all over it. A detective would say it has Satan's MO (method of operation). This song is musically beautiful. It has been performed by some of America's best-loved icons such as Frank Sinatra and Elvis Presley. If it were sung by screaming demons wearing T-shirts sporting severed goats' heads, even a child would be wary. But the messengers who have sung this song to America have been well loved. Yet the message is filled with the most potent poison in the universe. The theme of "My Way" embodies the heart of the "I will" philosophy of Satan. It ultimately was the venom that caused his fall and could cause your death as well. In stark contrast, the pure heart of the Christ-filled man echoes the words of Jesus as He faced death in the Garden of Gethsemane, saying, "Not my will, but Thy will be done."

JUST DO IT

TRY TO go one whole day without saying "I." It will be fun and tough, but worth the effort.

8

I₊ Woᴙᴅꜱ (ouʟᴅ Ꮶɪʟʟ

*All kinds of animals, birds, reptiles and creatures
of the sea are being tamed and have been tamed by
man, but no man can tame the tongue. It is a restless
evil, full of deadly poison.*

JAMES 3:7

PERHAPS THE BIGGEST CHALLENGE a Christian faces is taming his
tongue. There is no weapon as dangerous or as unmanageable.
For me it has been a particularly difficult task because I am a nat-
ural-born smart aleck. Words tend to roll off my tongue long before
I've had a chance to think about them. For instance, when I was a
teenager, the most heinous crime I could commit in my dad's book
was talking back. A smart response to either parent brought swift
and painful consequences. One night at the dinner table I casually
remarked that the biscuits could be better used as baseballs. Just as
my brain realized what my mouth had just spoken, the back of my
dad's hand came from behind his evening paper, catching me on
the chin and sending me tumbling backward.

The fact that you are even reading about this eruption should
give you an idea of how long ago it took place. If it had taken place
these days, I (of course) would have gotten up and immediately
called the Department of Human Services to report child abuse.
Horrified, they in turn would have promptly arrested my dad and
placed me under foster care. I would have then needed to leave
school early to make a living, preventing me from going to college.
Because that would have left me an uneducated, fatherless smart

aleck, I would have no doubt ended up flipping burgers instead of writing this book.

I'm not the only guy with foot-in-mouth disease; we all share it to a degree and deal with it differently. Christians sometimes disguise their lack of verbal self-control by making up their own little secret-code language. Any fluent speaker of Christianese knows that "bless his heart" means "he's a bumbling idiot." "I love him in the Lord" means "If it weren't for Jesus, I'd have to kill him." But a curse delivered even in Christian code does damage, if not to the uninformed listener, certainly to the speaker.

You've heard the saying, "If you don't have anything good to say, don't say anything." Well, my father-in-law lives by those words. I have never heard Bud say anything negative about anyone. Once, while chopping wood with my brother-in-law, I took a foolhardy bet. He said, "I'll bet you a Pepsi you can't get Bud to say anything negative about another person." I took the Pepsi challenge. As casually as possible, I said, "Bud, what do you think about Charles Manson, the mass murderer." To my disappointment, he set his ax down and after a pause said, "I guess he's all right, as long as they keep him in prison."

We would all do well to learn the art of pausing before speaking.

Is there a time to speak harshly? Sure there is. Jesus called the Pharisees snakes. He wasn't all that pleasant with the money-changers either. Jesus knew when to use His tongue like a dagger, but He also knew when to use it to heal. When sending the woman at the well (John 4) back to her village, He said, "Go and tell your husband and come back." The next paragraph reveals that Jesus knew all along the Samaritan woman wasn't married to the man in her house; in fact, he was her fifth lover. There are many self-righteous folks today who would have pounced on the opportunity to say, "Go get that other sinner you're shacking up with and come back here for a sermon on morality." Instead, Jesus spoke words of compassion that drew her into God's kingdom. The fire-and-brimstone approach might have had the opposite affect. Jesus didn't approve of her sin. He dealt with it with the kind of wisdom that brought her closer to God.

Just as a well-chosen word can bring life, a poorly chosen one can kill. Karen and Richard Carpenter sold millions of albums in the 1970s. She achieved the kind of fame and fortune most can only dream about. A thoughtless verbal jab, however, caused her to slowly kill herself at the age of thirty-two. She didn't do it all at once. Karen died as a result of anorexia nervosa. She had been devastated by a review that referred to her as "Richard's chubby sister." Words really can kill.

"Sticks and stones can break my bones, but words can never hurt me." This nursery-school rhyme is not altogether true. Words have more power than we think.

Celebrating the fiftieth anniversary of the end of World War II in Europe, Winston Churchill's grandson noted that his grandfather had never picked up a gun but may have done more to bring the war to a conclusion than any soldier. "My grandfather had the ability to mobilize words and send them into battle."

The tongue is an awesome weapon. The things we say can change people right before our eyes. But it's not only what we say that is important, sometimes what goes *unsaid* is just as powerful. A word of deserved praise that goes unspoken can fail to bring desperately needed healing to a wounded soul. An unspoken word of expected criticism can also restore a damaged spirit.

May the Lord give us the ability to use our tongues wisely.

JUST DO IT

FIND THE opportunity to encourage, thank, or praise five different people today. It's a habit worth developing.

9

CAUGHT

If we claim to be without sin, we deceive ourselves and the truth is not in us. If we confess our sins, he is faithful and just and will forgive us our sins and purify us from all unrighteousness.

1 JOHN 1:8–9

SEVERAL YEARS AGO MY FAMILY went through a difficult time. My uncle died of lung cancer, and that became the fuel for my mother's fierce anti-smoking campaign. She smelled my clothes every evening when I came in from being with my friends. My mom was tactful about it. She didn't just walk up and start smelling. She would always use a ploy like, "Come here, Dana, and give your mother a big hug." What are you gonna say? No, thanks? If she detected smoke, she would call in my dad to finish the interrogation. I'm thankful that my dad didn't sniff. He would just look me in the eye and say, "Dana, have you been smoking?" Gathering every bit of sincerity I could muster, I would look at him and say, "Who me? Smoke? Of course not." I'd lie in bed feeling like dirt for a couple of minutes, but by the next morning all was forgotten.

One night I was out with the boys at the video arcade making the universe a safer place, and the guys decide to step out for a smoke. We all went outside to suck on cigarettes and act tough. And just as I inhaled five cubic feet of tar, nicotine, and other killer pollutants, I turned around . . . and there was my dad. I'm not the brightest guy in the world, but I immediately knew I had three choices: (1) run, (2) say nothing and hope he went away, or (3) see if I could talk without exhaling.

I chose option three. It was a poor choice. With every sound I made, I looked like Puff the Magic Dragon. To my astonishment, my dad said nothing. He just got in his car and went home. When I came home I saw him sitting at the kitchen table, doing something I had never seen before. He was crying. This was my first experience of real guilt, and it made me want to die.

Conviction is an inescapable part of every Christian's life. That's good, but learning how to deal with it is critical. I remember the first time I read Psalm 51. King David had committed adultery with Bathsheba, Uriah's wife, then murdered Uriah, and had a son out of wedlock. Strangely, the first thing out of his mouth when confronted with his sin was, "Against you, [God] you only have I sinned." I remember thinking, *This was a weird attitude from someone who had caused so much human suffering.* Today, I realize that David understood something important about guilt: Forgiveness begins with a look to heaven first.

The apostle Paul tells us guilt can be broken down into two kinds of sorrow. One kind leads to life and forgiveness; the other brings death. The difference lies in the direction the eyes of guilt are looking. One looks to God and says, "Father, I have let you down again." The other looks inward and says, "I'm caught; now my life is really a mess" (2 Corinthians 7:10).

God-conscious sorrow brings life. Worldly sorrow actually leads away from genuine forgiveness because it doesn't acknowledge that all sin is against God. Second, it egotistically inflates the value of personal suffering. The best way to see these two types of conviction in operation is through the lives of Peter and Judas. Peter, hours after promising that he would die with Christ before he would deny Him, betrayed Him three times. Judas sold information about Christ's whereabouts to His enemies. Both men betrayed Jesus. Both experienced overwhelming sorrow. In fact, Judas actually gave the money back. But Peter is the one who turned back to God. Judas hanged himself.

Peter was given life and forgiveness because in his guilt he looked to the one offended. Judas hung himself because his sorrow was selfish. It may have been that he hated himself; it may have been that his life would never be the same. Or perhaps he couldn't live with the shame of being caught by his friends. Whatever the case, he preferred to gain absolution by punishing himself rather than bowing at the foot of the cross.

Judas's self-inflicted punishment was either an act of ignorance or arrogance. If he thought that his death would somehow clear the slate, he either overvalued himself or undervalued the price of sin. Godly sorrow looks to heaven first because only God has the right and the ability to forgive sin. All sin is against an infinitely holy God, therefore, no sinful, finite man could ever pay for it.

Complete forgiveness only comes by looking upward, never inward. Sure, we may feel terrible. We may even experience embarrassment or rejection, but these feelings fall infinitely short of being adequate punishment for our sin. Only the perfect Lamb of God is the commensurate payment. To think that the negative consequences of our sin, whether fact or feeling, help to right the scales is an indication that we greatly overestimate our own value . . . or we greatly underestimate what sin costs.

Our sin is first and foremost against God. If we desire to be free from the paralyzing sorrow that comes with the awareness of sin, we must first tearfully bow to Him, then prove that we truly value Christ and His sacrifice more than anything in the universe by rising up and going forward in forgiveness without as much as a second thought.

By the way, the night I was caught smoking turned out to be a blessing in disguise. My father didn't punish me. Instead, we sat up until late into the night and just talked. In fact, we spent a lot more time talking after that evening. Dad turned out to be a pretty good listener, and I learned how to be a lot more honest.

JUST DO IT

GET ON your knees in a private place and confess your sins out loud to God. Then spend a moment praising Jesus for paying for those sins on the cross.

10
CHRISTA

Though he slay me, yet will I hope in him.

JOB 13:15

ON JANUARY 28, 1986, NASA launched the first civilian into space. Christa McAulliffe was a thirty-seven-year-old high-school teacher and mother of three. The nation, her class, and her family looked on with pride and anticipation. As the space shuttle *Challenger* made a routine liftoff, Christa's classroom of ninth graders led the country in a cheer via national television.

The cheers quickly turned to silent bewilderment and then to sobbing as all soon realized that something had gone drastically wrong. Seventy-three seconds into the flight, *Challenger* disappeared in a ball of yellow and white fire. Debris scattered in all directions, taking a million different paths back to Earth. The protective pod that held the passenger and crew fell to the sea at 190 miles per hour.

Helpless to do anything and knowing the impossibility of survival, the last transmission from *Challenger*'s pilot was simply, "Uh, oh." As millions watched on television, they hoped that death was instantaneous for Christa and the crew aboard *Challenger*. Months later, however, we learned that death came three eternal minutes later for at least three members of the crew.

All eight passengers carried an emergency airpack. Four were recovered by navy divers; three of them had been turned on manually after the explosion, each of the three showed about three minutes of air consumed. We can only imagine what thoughts might have filled those last 180 seconds.

The *Challenger* disaster was a tremendous blow to the invulnerable, we-can-do-anything reputation of NASA. A Congressional investigation was launched, and the finger-pointing began. Soon experts were focusing on the giant O-rings that held the rocket's solid-fuel tanks together. Apparently, some bad decisions were made regarding the launch in bad weather, as well.

The explanations have meaning for future civilians in space but do little to heal the wounds of the past. Nothing will erase the picture of that classroom of horrified ninth graders. For families and friends, no Congressional report will fill the hollow feeling left by that final "Uh, oh."

If any good has come to us in the *Challenger* catastrophe, perhaps it's a reminder that life is short and even the brilliant minds of NASA cannot guarantee our safety. Difficult days are coming to all of us. They span a wide expanse in severity and finality, but they do inevitably come. Invariably, they leave us searching for answers and asking why. The investigation into the *Challenger* explosion told us what happened, but only God knows why.

A world without God can only hope to answer the question of what, never why. In a godless world, tragedies have no meaning. But in a world where Christ rules, no event—small or gigantic—comes without a purpose. Through faith in a loving, all-wise God, we have the confidence that every terrible "what" has an excellent "why." It is far easier to leave our grief and confusion at the feet of the Savior when we know both that Jesus has felt this pain and He would never allow it to touch us without good reason. We may not be able to see the purpose now, but something about the tender compassion of Jesus tells me there are explanations awaiting us in eternity.

JUST DO IT

Do you have any confusion or bitterness about a loved one who has been taken away from you by death or divorce. Write a letter that you don't intend to mail to the person you miss. Tell them your feelings. Then write one addressed to Jesus. Be honest.

11
DOCTOR DEATH

Satan himself masquerades as an angel of light.
2 CORINTHIANS 11:14

VE WENT TO WORK IN THE GARDEN of God just as she had done every day from the beginning. She had caretaking to do, and, besides, the garden was beautiful and exhilarating.

The first order of business was to catch a glimpse of the daybreak gleaming through the special trees. Then Eve would get on with her work.

When she arrived at the center of the garden, there was someone, or should I say some*thing* already there. It was the serpent, one of the most intelligent and lovely of all the animals in God's garden.

"Hello, Eve," the serpent said. "I've been waiting for you. You're so busy, but I wanted to make sure you noticed that the fruit on this tree has ripened. I wouldn't want you to miss having a little taste before the summer heat causes it to go bad."

Eve, obviously a bit startled, blurted out, "Thanks for your concern, but I couldn't. I mean, I mustn't."

"Oh, come now," the serpent said. "Did God really say you couldn't eat the fruit from these beautiful trees? Did you hear Him say it, or is that just another thing that Adam told you? You've got to remember that it's been a while now since Adam was made. There's a good chance he has the whole matter confused."

Sounding a little defensive, Eve replied, "We can eat some of the fruit. In fact, we can eat from any tree we want except for these two. Adam says that God told him right to his face we mustn't eat or even touch it or we will die."

"You won't die," the snake snapped. "Come a little closer, and I'll let you in on a little secret." Looking around to make sure they were alone, the strange creature hissed, "Eve, my poor naive human friend, don't you know that it's this special fruit that makes God so smart? One little bite and you'll know good and evil just like the Big Guy. You wanna be like God, don't you, Eve? I know I do."

Eve was dying for a taste. If that fruit was only half as good as it looked, it would most certainly be the best thing she had ever tasted. And anyway, it would make her wise like God. Growing more like Him was something God Himself had said was important. This wasn't exactly the way He had planned, but it got there just the same, and as far as Eve was concerned, the sooner the better.

Eve made up her mind to do it. To the snake's delight, she took the fruit into her hands and put it to her lips. Her heart raced as she swallowed the first bite. To her surprise it tasted no better than the fruit of the other trees. By this time Adam was reaching for a piece, too. Thus Adam and Eve became the world's first assisted-suicide victims. Oh, they didn't know it yet. You can't see a soul die. The only way you can tell if the soul is dead is by circumstantial evidence, like behavior. We all know that bodies die a little bit at a time. So it took Eve and Adam a while to figure out that they had indeed killed themselves, just as God had warned.

Today there are a number of books that deal with spiritual warfare. They tell stories of people speaking with bizarre voices, untouched objects moving across rooms, and screaming demons. I'm not saying that those things don't happen, but they rate low on the list of real Christian dangers. More often when Satan comes to tempt, the situation will be quite the opposite. He will speak by way of someone or something that causes you no fear. After all, healthy fear is God's warning mechanism, and Satan will want to avoid your antennas going up.

At least at first he probably won't demand that you fall down and worship him. He'll use his two tools, the world and the flesh, and he will tell you that what you *desire* is something you *deserve*. It's really just a tiny shortcut to what God wanted you to have in the first place. "Go ahead, get a copy of those answers to the test. You'd have had more time to study if it weren't for that choir program coming up at church," or "Who will care if you have sex on prom night. God created sex as part of nature."

Satan works this way because he has no choice. He can't kill you on his own. He can only do what God permits. He's forced to operate like a nether-world version of Dr. Jack Kevorkian. He tells you that you are missing something or that you've been unfairly deprived. Then, in a warm caring voice, he simply lays before you the tools you need to kill yourself.

JUST DO IT

SPEND YOUR prayer time searching for the areas where you feel deprived. How might Satan tempt you in those areas?

12
LUCKY US

He made the earth by his power; he founded the world by his wisdom and stretched out the heavens by his understanding.

JEREMIAH 51:15

SOME THINGS HAPPEN IN LIFE THAT SEEM too odd to be coincidence. For instance, the Kennedy-Lincoln list that has been widely circulated. Abraham Lincoln became president in 1860. John Kennedy was elected in 1960. Lincoln's secretary was named Kennedy; Kennedy's secretary was named Lincoln. Both died of gunshot wounds to the back of the head on a Friday. Lincoln's assassin shot him in a theater and was captured in a warehouse. Kennedy's assassin shot him from a warehouse and was captured in a theater. Booth and Oswald were both killed before they could stand trial. Lincoln was succeeded by Andrew Johnson, born in 1808; Kennedy was succeeded by Lyndon Johnson, born in 1908. The names Lincoln and Kennedy each contain seven letters. Andrew Johnson and Lyndon Johnson contain thirteen letters. John Wilkes Booth and Lee Harvey Oswald each contain fifteen letters. Can this be just a curious twist of fate?

Paul Harvey tells the story of a fateful Wednesday evening choir practice scheduled at West Side Baptist Church in Beatrice, Nebraska. Eighteen people were scheduled to be there at 7:30 sharp. Had they been, all would have been killed. The furnace had a natural gas leak, which caused an explosion that demolished the whole church. It occurred at exactly 7:30. By a strange twist of fate, none of the eighteen were there. One had fallen asleep.

Another, who was scheduled to pick up two others, had car trouble. Even the pastor was late because his wristwatch was five minutes slow. Something prevented each of them from being on time.

Strange things do happen. Some call it luck, but Christians must call it divine providence because, in reality, there is no such thing as luck. God is behind every tiny detail of life. Proverbs says, "The lot is cast into the lap, but its every decision is from the LORD" (Proverbs 16:33). Luck believes in a random, godless universe. It is a concept that is embraced by default by those who have no better explanation for the odd coincidences of life. Sometimes God does that which makes even the most optimistic believers in luck look rather silly. Yet many still cling to the notion of a godless, random universe because the alternative is too difficult to bear.

Most of academia teach that our world began with a Big Bang. This cosmic event created an environment on earth that was favorable toward creating life. Somewhere on earth was an organic soup from which you and I owe our origin. The theory is that somehow amino acids came together in just the right sequence and formed enzymes (the proteins that are catalysts for chemical reactions). These enzymes in turn came together to form bacteria, and before you know it, presto, here we were.

The problem with this scenario is that amino acids have to come together in a precise sequence to form an enzyme, and it takes two thousand functioning enzymes to form one bacterium. This process is so complex that scientists have not been able to do it, even under the best laboratory conditions. Mathematics may provide us with some insight as to why.

Statisticians have calculated that the chances of this event taking place at random are one in ten multiplied by the forty-thousandth power. To give you an idea of how big this number is, it is estimated that there are only ten to the eightieth power atoms in the known universe! If it is chance that brought us here, we have defied such unbelievable odds that to call us the luckiest people in the universe would be a huge understatement. These odds are so laughable that some scientists have concluded that the reason this theory is not abandoned by the scientific community must be psychological rather than scientific. Any theory that has less chance of happening than a blindfolded man picking a specific atom out of a hat the size of the universe is ridiculous science.

We might find all this humorous if it were not for the anti-God predisposition being created by academia. From Carl Sagan to the local high-school chemistry teacher, these impossible odds are widely acknowledged in the science and education community but not widely taught. A coverup of sorts is in progress because little glitches like these make the science world look silly. This very day unsuspecting schoolchildren will be taught a scientific theory that is virtually a statistical impossibility. Teachers will explain how we evolved from organic soup as if it has been scientifically proven. Yet the opposite is true, and the reason why is clear. They have no other alternative but God.

My university professor once remarked, "It takes a little faith to believe in evolution." He was wrong. It takes a lot of faith. Evolution science is in realty the religion of evolution superstition, and many prefer to ask this system of blind faith to come into their hearts and avoid God. Those who trust in a random universe take a cosmic gamble on improbable odds with incomprehensible consequences if they are wrong. What is worse is that they encourage others to follow in their footsteps. With the passion of an evangelist, they lead the way to the only truly godless part of our universe, Hell.

Jeremiah says, "He made the earth by his power; he founded the world by his wisdom and stretched out the heavens by his understanding" (Jeremiah 51:15). This is an explanation for our being here that requires far less faith and gives us far more confidence that the events of our lives are in the capable hands of an incredible master designer.

JUST DO IT

THERE ARE many fine books written by Bible-believing scientists. Pick one up (when you're finished with this one) so you'll be armed with the true scientific truth about creation:

- Ashby L. Camp, *The Myth of Natural Origins* (Tempe, Ariz.: Ktisis Pub.), 1994.
- Marvin L. Lubenow, *Bones of Contention* (Grand Rapids, Mich.: Baker Book House), 1992.

- James Porter Moreland, *Christianity and the Nature of Science* (Grand Rapids, Mich.: Baker Book House), 1989.
- Henry Madison Morris, *The Genesis Record* (Grand Rapids: Baker Book House), 1976.

13
SHEEP

*If anyone chooses to do God's will, he will find
out whether my teaching comes from God.*

JOHN 7:17

ANIMAL COMPARISONS MAKE POWERFUL analogies. Call somebody
a snake, without even saying what kind, and you'd better duck.
Football and basketball teams are nicknamed "Lions" and "Bulls"
in the hope that the personality of the team will reflect the nature
of that animal. That's why you wouldn't call your team the Texas
Turkeys or the Saint Louis Skunks. Mascots, like pictures, are
worth a thousand words.

The Bible frequently uses animal names to tell a story quickly
and powerfully: the devil is a dragon, Jesus is the Lion of Judah.
Guess what you and I are: sheep. More than 750 times the Bible
mentions sheep, and in nearly half of those references God is
describing His people. This is not entirely good news.

Sheep are an accurate comparison but not necessarily a flat-
tering one. In Psalm 23, David says, "He leads me beside quiet
waters." The shepherd has to find still water because some sheep
are so frightened of bubbling water that they will die of thirst rather
than approach it. Isaiah adds more insight into the character of
sheep saying, "All we like sheep have gone astray." Sheep have a
tendency to graze while paying no attention to their surroundings.
It is not unusual for a lamb to walk right off a cliff. Sheep are not
only dumb, they are practically defenseless. Goats when attacked

by wolves form a tight circle, protecting one another. Sheep scatter and are easily picked off one at a time.

Sheep may be the only animal on the planet that are so fearful and stupid that they require constant care to survive. Yet God has given them two gifts to ensure that they will always receive the supervision they need. First, He has given them the desire to follow their shepherd. Second, He has given them the ability to recognize the shepherd's voice.

In ancient Israel, when a shepherd needed to go into town for supplies, he had to pack up the whole flock and march them into town. The shepherd would enter by a special gate, ingeniously called the sheep gate. Here, in one big pen, all visiting shepherds would leave their flocks. Perhaps it occurs to you that this might present a problem when it was time to leave. The sheep weren't tagged or even counted, yet their shepherds had no difficulty leaving with exactly those animals they came with. Here's why: Sheep form an incredible bond with their shepherd. Whether it is from love or an intuitive knowledge of their dependence, sheep long to be near their shepherds. Consequently, shepherds don't walk behind their flock, prodding them onward. They just take off walking and the sheep follow.

The other amazing gift is the sheep's ability to recognize the voice of the shepherd. When time came to leave the city sheep pen, the shepherd simply uttered his call, turned, and headed back to the fields. Incredibly, each of his—and only his—lambs followed.

Jesus is our shepherd and we are His sheep. "He calls his own sheep by name and leads them out. When he has brought out all his own, he goes on ahead of them, and his sheep follow him because they know his voice. But they will never follow a stranger; in fact, they will run away from him because they do not recognize a stranger's voice" (John 10:3–5).

There is no question that Christ's followers are supernaturally able to recognize His voice above the cacophony of would-be messiahs who call. No other voice captures their attention or comforts them like His. This is an amazing gift of the Spirit granted to the flock that calls Jesus of Nazareth its shepherd. But it is not a gift that can be taken for granted or neglected. The longer and nearer we live with the shepherd, the easier it is to recognize His voice. Likewise, the further we wander away from the sound of His voice, the more difficult it is to hear His voice. Sheep that develop disobedient feet also develop ears that are dull of hearing.

If you wish to know the will of God, you must first be willing to obey it.

JUST DO IT

SPEND YOUR prayer time listing those people, places, and things that divert your attention from the shepherd. Confess your sin and ask the Lord to improve your hearing.

14

(OULD JESUS LOSE HIS HAMMER?

For we do not have a high priest who is unable to sympathize with our weaknesses, but we have one who has been tempted in every way, just as we are—yet was without sin.

HEBREWS 4:15

I LOVE TO ASK BIBLE STUDY GROUPS theoretical questions and sit back and listen. My favorite is, "While Jesus was on earth, was it possible for Him to lose His hammer?" I've heard some pretty strange answers to this question, but the best, by far, came from my father-in-law. He replied, "I guess He could have if He wanted to."

That answer is 100 percent on the theological money. Not only could Jesus chose to have the ability to lose His hammer, but that's what He wanted. Here's why.

The ability to lose His hammer made Jesus a more perfect savior. Philippians 2:6–7 says Jesus, "Who, being in very nature God, did not consider equality with God something to be grasped, but made himself nothing, taking the very nature of a servant." In what sense did Jesus make Himself nothing? The King James Version uses the word "emptied" in place of the word "nothing." Was His nature changed? No, He emptied Himself of the right to express His divine nature with His omni-attributes (all powerful, all-knowing, always present). In other words, the almighty, all-knowing Lord of the universe became a normal man of limited strength and mental ability.

As a child, Jesus "grew in wisdom" as He read the Scripture and learned of His messianic mission (Luke 2:52). Hebrews 5:8 tells us that, "Although he was a son, he learned obedience from what he suffered." He often prayed to God to know His will. So it's clear that Jesus did some learning while He was here in human form—and He just might have prayed once or twice to learn the whereabouts of a missing hammer.

Now, this is not to say that Jesus wasn't superior to us in wisdom and power. He obviously knew something we couldn't. For example, John 18:4 tells us He knew in advance the events and details that would surround His death. He also knew details about the adulterous life of the woman at the well. But on the other hand, He told His disciples the hour of His Second Coming, telling them, "No one knows about that day or hour, not even the angels in heaven, nor the Son, but only the Father" (Matthew 24:36).

Whether or not Christ could have lost His hammer is more than just hypothetical gymnastics, it's important to us for three reasons. First, Jesus' life demonstrates the power of an ordinary, yet sinless man. When Jesus calmed the wind and waves or fed the five thousand, he demonstrated what we might have been had Adam not have fallen. It gives us a strong incentive not to further dilute the power of God by succumbing to the lure of sin.

Second, a truly human Jesus is a better role model. A Jesus who is omniscient and all-powerful seems to be playing on an uneven field. Our temptation is to say, "Sure, it's easy for You to be brave, You can always use Your divine strength to save Yourself," or "Of course You're not worried about the future because You know every detail of it." Jesus relied on God in the same way He has taught us. We can honestly say that what Jesus told us to do, He demonstrated, but not with any power that is unavailable to you or me.

Finally, a fully human Jesus is more accessible to you and me. Maybe it's because misery loves company, but it's reassuring to me when I'm searching for my car keys that Jesus must have experienced similar frustrations. He has truly walked in our shoes. That makes it more amazing that He was able to live a life without sin . . . and it makes me want to try all the harder to be like Him.

JUST DO IT

SPEND YOUR prayer time reflecting on how much more of God's power might flow through your life if it were not for sin. Spend some time in confession as well as praise, thanking Jesus for doing what we are unable to.

15
LIVING SACRIFICES

Therefore, I urge you, brothers, in view of God's mercy, to offer your bodies as living sacrifices, holy and pleasing to God—this is your spiritual act of worship.
ROMANS 12:1

I LOVE OXYMORONS. YOU KNOW, those little phrases where two opposite words are put together like "my sweet sorrow" or "military intelligence." One that always gets my attention is when the flight attendant says, "In the event of a water landing." I'm always thinking that if we end up getting wet, it will be because we had a water "crash."

The greatest oxymoron in the Bible is found in Romans 12:1 where we are described as "living sacrifices." Sacrifices in the Old Testament were skinned, sliced, and then burnt at the altar. They were anything but "living." Yet the Bible describes Christians as living sacrifices, and it is for a good reason. Unlike slaughtered lambs or bulls, we have the ability to crawl down off the altar.

I grew up in a little southern church that regularly sang "I Have Decided to Follow Jesus." The chorus ends with "no turning back, no turning back." I wish this were so. In reality, we turn back regularly. For even the "righteous man falls seven times" and finds himself having to crawl back up on God's altar.

In 1519 there was a great Spanish military leader named Hernando Cortés. The king of Spain ordered him to conquer Mexico, and Cortés did. The invasion began at Vera Cruz with a relatively tiny invasion force of just seven hundred men. The first thing Cortés did upon offloading his men in Mexico was to burn and sink his eleven ships, thus providing no means of retreat. When the natives saw this do-or-die commitment, they began laying down their weapons.

Because of our ongoing battle with sin and self, we always have the option to retreat. That is why Jesus told His disciples, "If anyone would come after me, he must deny himself and take up his cross daily and follow me" (Luke 9:23).

No one knew better the pain of crucifixion than first-century Christians. They were eyewitnesses, in fact, many were unwilling participants. Although the pain was considerable, at least the victim could only be tortured once. But the disciple of Christ must torture his selfish will "daily."

Sometimes Christians speak of this event as a rededication, but rededication is far too beautiful a description for the painful recrucifixion that must take place in the Christian's life. Every new morning we must echo the apostle Paul's declaration, "I die every day" (1 Corinthians 15:31). Daily, we "living sacrifices" must determine to place our lives on the altar of God and *remain there.* For it is only on the altar that we are pleasing to God and useful in His service.

JUST DO IT

WHAT AREAS of your life need to visit the sacrificial altar? Make a list of problem areas and prayerfully offer them before Christ's throne. Remember to tear this list up and put it in the trash where it belongs.

16
ANGELS AND WINNEBAGOS

"See that you do not look down on one of these little ones. For I tell you that their angels in heaven always see the face of my Father in heaven."

MATTHEW 18:10

ONE OF THE STRANGEST CHAPTERS of the Bible is Daniel 10. The Bible was written to help us live godly lives, so it doesn't say a lot about what goes on in the unseen world of angels. Daniel 10 stands out as one of those rare glimpses.

An angel appears to Daniel and says, "Since the first day that you set your mind to gain understanding and to humble yourself before your God, your words were heard, and I have come in response to them. But the prince of the Persian kingdom resisted me twenty-one days. Then Michael, one of the chief princes, came to help me, because I was detained there with the king of Persia" (verses 12–13).

It seems clear that the king of Persia is no ordinary man. The Old Testament tells us that in one night an angel killed 185,000 Assyrians. So I don't think a human could have much luck restraining this messenger of God. What must be described here is a battle between superbeings. The mind races with the possibilities of what may be going on just beyond our eyesight. I'm tempted to say that I wish Daniel 10 had given us more specifics, but, on the other hand, those details may be more than I want to know.

When things started going relatively well for DeGarmo and Key, we sold our old Chevy truck and bought a five-year-old

Winnebago. It was like heaven. You could actually sleep in it, provided it wasn't your turn to drive or that you weren't in the Northeast. I guess it's because of the hard winters up there, but sometimes it's tough to tell if you were driving on an interstate or in the Baja 500.

The old Winnebago was as ugly as a mud fence, but it had three great sleeping places. There were two padded couches, a nice warm spot on the floor just above the transmission, and the notorious "psycho bunk."

When we first bought the new wagon, this particular bunk was one of the main attractions. Of course, it wasn't called the psycho bunk then, that came later. This bed was suspended from the ceiling. It was intended to be used by lowering it and locking it into position after the camper was safely parked. We quickly discovered that it wasn't much fun to sleep in while the Winnebago was rolling. This process of discovery is how it got its name.

You see, the psycho bunk rocked back and forth with the movements of the camper, but not like a rolling ship. It was much worse. This one moved freely in every direction, side to side and up and down. Once I remarked after climbing out of it, "This is what it must feel like to be losing your mind." Eventually, the psycho bunk was used only for storage.

On one particular occasion, the psycho bunk almost killed me. It was after an all-night run. I curled up in my favorite spot on the floor just under it. T.C. and Tony sat reading inches away. The bunk was stacked high with spare lighting parts and tools. I was directly underneath, sound asleep.

With no warning, someone yelled into my ear, "Look out!" As you can imagine, the scream caused an immediate involuntary response. I sat up like I was spring-loaded. Just as I rose from the floor, a large crate of metal parts crashed and broke into a million pieces exactly where my head had been just milliseconds before.

I looked up to Tony and T.C., both of them were as white as a sheet. We said nothing for a long moment. We all just stared at one another. It was clear that we were each trying to figure out what had happened. I broke the silence. "Man, guys, that was close, whoever it was who yelled gets dinner on me." T.C. said,

"Dana, nobody made a sound. We thought you were asleep. You jumped up like you were trying to scare us or something. That box smashed where your head was, but we didn't hear a thing."

Looking at the dent in the floor, it occurred to me that somewhere in that camper I had an invisible pal. Someone was looking out for me, and as I thought it over, it made me feel good.

The world we see is a dangerous place. There is terrorism, crime, and war. We can only guess what the unseen world of angels is like. One thing is clear, God's invisible servants are busy. Thank the Lord their business is taking care of you and me.

JUST DO IT

THERE IS nothing to do here other than pause to thank God for His love and concern for us.

17
Go Ahead and Jump

Now to him who is able to do immeasurably more than all we ask or imagine, according to his power that is at work within us.

EPHESIANS 3:20

KARL WALLENDA WAS THE Babe Ruth of aerialists. Once, as a promotional gimmick, he walked a high wire two hundred feet above Niagara Falls. When onlookers noticed a man walking confidently over the rocks and water, they began to cheer wildly. One wrong step would mean certain death.

Karl walked out to the halfway point and then back. Laying aside his balance beam, he took a wheelbarrow and pushed it across the high wire as the crowd shouted their approval. Karl quickly made his way back to the hysterical crowd and said, "Ladies and gentlemen, do you think I can put a person in this wheelbarrow and push it to the other side?" The crowd went wild with affirmation. Then Karl asked that now-famous question, "Who will volunteer?" As the crowd fell silent, one little voice spoke up and said, "I will."

What the audience and press didn't know was that Karl knew no one would volunteer but the little girl. The little girl had been told to volunteer. She was Karl's daughter, so she was more than willing to comply. She knew her daddy could safely push her across the high wire. He had done it dozens of times before in other cities.

When I was ten, I used to climb a tree that allowed me to see all over Memphis. The very first time I climbed it was nearly my last. My mother called me in for dinner, and it was only then I realized that I couldn't get down. My sister, responding to Mom's dinner call, walked underneath the tree. Seeing my predicament, she offered to catch me if I would jump. Now, my relationship to Jo Lyn was what you might expect between a little brother and a big sister. We fought constantly, and I didn't trust her any farther than I could throw a house. Even if I thought she was willing to catch me, I didn't think she was able. So I stayed in the tree till I starved to death. Just kidding, my dad came and got me down.

The Wallenda story and my tree experience are two sides of the same coin. Karl's daughter obeyed her father and got into the wheelbarrow because of three things:

1. She was told to.

2. She believed her father was willing to keep her safe.

3. She knew he was able.

In my case, I received a promise from my sister, but I was quite confident that she was neither willing nor able to perform her promise. Some say that faith is blind. What they mean by that is that faith is sometimes not based on common sense. What they're describing, however, is not biblical faith, but rather superstition. Real faith is based on good solid information and therefore makes great sense.

Christians must never leap without answering three questions. These answers form the three links of a chain that can hold us securely above the deepest chasm of doubt. The first link is answering this question: "Has God asked me to jump?" The second is, "Is God willing to catch me?" The final link is, "Is He able to do what He has promised?" When we know we've heard His voice, trust He loves us, and are confident that He rules the world, leaps of faith are a piece of cake. Though we dangle over the Grand Canyon of doubt, we can rest in the confidence we are held firmly by this unbreakable three-link chain of faith.

If Satan is ever successful in causing us to fall into doubt and despair, it will come because we questioned God's willingness or ability to rescue us. The serpent was not able to shipwreck Eve's faith until he successfully got her to think twice about God's character. He made it sound as if God was being selfish in keeping the fruit and its power to Himself saying, "God knows that when you eat of it your eyes will be opened, and you will be like God, knowing good and evil" (Genesis 3:5). When Eve doubted God's character, the chain of faith was broken and that started her fall.

Peter, on the other hand, was challenged by other circumstances to question God's ability. As Jesus was coming toward the disciples on the Sea of Galilee, Peter went out on the water to join Him. Getting out of the boat, the disciple began to sink when he perceived the immensity of the storm around him and began to wonder if Christ was great enough to save him from it. Enduring faith is built on the confidence that Jesus wants what is best for you and is able to provide it.

When you have this point of view, following Him into a storm or over a cliff becomes reasonable behavior. It may not look like it to those who haven't heard His voice, don't know His heart, and haven't witnessed His eternal power, but leaps of faith are very sane when you're leaping at the request of the one who was "able" to speak the universe into existence and was "willing" to take your place on a cross.

JUST DO IT

WRITE THESE verses on a note card and tape it some place where you can't miss it, like the bathroom mirror.

> *"I am the LORD, the God of all mankind. Is anything too hard for me?"*
>
> JEREMIAH 32:27

> *And without faith it is impossible to please God, because anyone who comes to him must believe that he exists and that he rewards those who earnestly seek him.*
>
> HEBREWS 11:6

18
More Than Words

We know that we have come to know him if we obey his commands.

1 John 2:3

If we examine the history of man's nature as an individual, we are constantly observing that that spark of divinity in his breast, the longing for what is good is being extinguished by the flame of desire and greed. Our hearts, reason and the word of Christ all call out to us loudly and convincingly to tell us that union with Christ is absolutely necessary, that without Him we would be utterly forsaken of God, for apart from Him we can do nothing.

THESE WORDS SO ELOQUENTLY EXPRESS our need and total dependency on Jesus. As a somewhat jealous writer, I was amazed to learn they were penned by a boy of seventeen named Karl Marx—the founder of communism! This wasn't all that Karl wrote. He continued his writing career with a book entitled *Das Kapital*. This book is regarded as the communist bible. Some historians estimate that as result of the philosophy in this book more than two hundred million people have lost their lives.

At seventeen, Marx seemed so near the household of faith. Some would have even considered him in it. Yet Marx only gave the appearance of believing. Marx never completed the walk toward saving faith.

Faith is made up of three essential steps: acknowledging the truth, accepting its reliability, then acting in accordance with what you've heard. One must hear and understand the facts of the gospel, agree with their essential truthfulness, then demonstrate that those truths have taken root by outward manifestations of faith.

Unbelievers fall into one of two categories, those who say they believe the facts of the gospel but don't, and those who say they don't believe the gospel and are telling the truth. Here we are concerned primarily with the first group, those who say they believe but do not.

Knowing the facts of the gospel and even making an eloquent profession of faith are not enough. You might object and remind me of Romans 10:9, "If you confess with your mouth, 'Jesus is Lord,' and believe in your heart that God raised him from the dead, you will be saved." I'd say there is an eternity of difference between knowing the facts and believing them.

Consider the example of this famous female pop singer. Just before her Detroit concert she prayed: "Dear Lord, it seems like every time I'm standing in this circle before the show, I'm asking for something extra special. And they say, 'ask and ye shall receive,' so I'm begging you to give me a voice to sing with this evening. Amen."

These could have been the words heard before any Christian concert, but far from singing to glorify God, this superstar blasphemed Him. Immediately following her prayer she stepped out on the stage and for the next hour and a half performed simulated sex acts. She proudly displayed a crucifix, saying, "She likes the thought of having a naked man between her breasts."

This person probably knows the facts of the gospel but has clearly never accepted them as true. No matter what she says with her mouth, her works betray her profession of faith. Her behavior is an unmistakable symptom of a deep-rooted problem.

There is an old story of a turtle and a scorpion facing a swollen river. The scorpion says to the turtle, "If you take me across on your back, I promise not to sting you." Reasoning that if the scorpion did sting him, he would surely drown, the turtle agreed. Halfway across the river the turtle felt the deadly scorpion's sting. Just before he died, the turtle looked back at the scorpion and asked, "Why did you do that?" As the scorpion and the turtle began to sink, he answered, "I can't help it. I'm a scorpion and that's my nature."

Scorpions act like scorpions because they can act no other way. While believers are compelled to practice righteousness because they believe, unbelievers must act out their unbelief. They are bound by their nature; to be free of it, they must do more than acknowledge the truth of the gospel. They must embrace it and obey it.

Perhaps you're asking, "Who are you to judge another person's fate?" I'd reply, "I don't judge anyone's destiny at all, just their fruit." The Scripture says that we should judge a tree by its fruit. So then, we are nothing more than fruit inspectors, and right now this confused young lady's fruit is looking like a hothouse tomato, nice and red on the outside but mushy in the middle. My fruit inspection has no effect on where she spends eternity, other than the chance that I might alert her to the fact that faith without works is dead, because faith without works is not faith at all.

It is eternally tragic to gloss over this important truth to spare hurt feelings. If I see that a person's deeds are not harmonizing with his words, and I give him confidence that his faith is genuine, I may be giving that person a false sense of security that he will take with him to hell. John said, "But if anyone obeys his word, God's love is truly made complete in him. This is how we know we are in him" (1 John 2:5). Security grows as we see ourselves living in harmony with our new obedient nature—and security should languish if we do not.

Again you might say, "Don't believers sometimes sin," and I would say yes, they do commit sins, but they do not *practice* sin. In other words, they do not sin as a lifestyle because they inwardly hate sin and it is an uncomfortable, unnatural state of being.

The righteous man falls seven times, but he rises again and again (Proverbs 24:16). The wicked man stumbles and stays down. The normal condition of the righteous man is standing. When he occasionally falls, he gets up. The normal place you would expect to see the wicked man is in a fallen condition. He is like the commercial where the lady says, "I've fallen and I can't get up." You may occasionally mistake the righteous for the wicked if you observe them at one of those unusual times when they have stumbled, but if you continue to observe you'll soon see them get up and shake the dust off. They do it because that's what believers do.

How is your fruit? Do your words and actions agree? Does your lifestyle indicate that there is a believer inside that vessel of flesh? If your behavior is causing you to have a little healthy skepticism about the direction you're headed, maybe that's a good thing. Better to find yourself in heaven surprised, than go to hell feeling secure.

JUST DO IT

SET ASIDE fifteen minutes today for a quiet time of self-examination.

19
A BRIDGE TOO FAR

So God created man in his own image, in the image
of God he created him; male and female he created them.
GENESIS 1:27

AS A COLLEGE STUDENT, I HAD assumed that faith and science were like the musical styles of Hank Williams Jr. and Beethoven—not at all related. These days I have come to realize just how much "faith" it takes to accept Darwin's theory of evolution.

Even a casual seeker of human origins must soon come to the four great chasms on Darwin's path of natural selection. Each of these great gulfs requires bridges of blind faith to proceed from the Big Bang to mankind.

First is the bridge from death to life, or put another way, from the inanimate to the animate. How much faith does it take to believe that the right conditions accidentally occurred at just the precise moment in time that allowed lightning (or something) to strike a pool of prehistoric goop and, presto, some living thing appeared? Now, in order to hang around, this new organism would have needed to have been zapped complete with a digestive system, so it could sustain itself, and a very clever reproductive system. To continue up the hill of natural selection, this new whatever must have the ability to produce offspring stronger and better than the original. Otherwise, this new life would have quickly disappeared.

The second bridge requires us to cross the fixed nature of the species. Genesis says that each species was designed to reproduce "after its own kind." This is not to say that species don't adapt to their environments, but it is to say that frogs don't become birds no matter how convenient it might be for them to fly. A man a million years ago may have been shorter or even hairier, but he was still a man.

Scientists have accumulated millions of fossils, yet not one fossil bridges a gap between species. The search for these missing links has become the Holy Grail for evolutionists and has been totally unsuccessful.

The third leap of faith is over the laws of thermodynamics. The second law states that things run down without outside help. Nature moves from organization to disorganization. Which means that without the intervention of some intelligent life, no matter how long you wait, your room will never clean itself.

Finally, how does evolution account for the spiritual side of humans as it concerns things that have nothing to do with surviving? The forces that drive Darwin's theory of natural selection would have little use for art or music. Survival of the fittest could never have produced people with a deep sense of conscience or willingness to sacrifice.

Ten thousand years from now a shark will still not have a conscience, but oceanographers will protect them. Dogs will not paint Mona Lisas, but veterinarians will still mend their broken bones.

I have to say that the way the Bible tells it still makes far more sense than the hole-ridden theory left to us by Darwin. Maybe Darwin thought that by now we could have established those bridges required to give his theory believability. Yet, after all these years, "In the beginning God created the heavens and the earth" makes more sense and requires far less faith.

JUST DO IT

EXPLORE YOUR creative side. Prayerfully sing your favorite praise and worship song, thanking God for a world filled with art and music. If this applies, ask the Lord to give you renewed dedication to learn those guitar chords, write that poetry, call about those painting lessons, join your church's drama group or choir. If you're not the "arty" type, visit an art gallery or buy concert tickets. Trust me. It will be good for you.

20

WHERE'S MY SPIRITUAL GIFT?

Since you are eager to have spiritual gifts, try to excel in gifts that build up the church.

1 CORINTHIANS 14:12

RONNIE STEVENS TOOK OVER AS PASTOR of a large southern church after spending eight years ministering in Moscow and other Eastern European cities. Things had changed a lot in America, especially in the world of technology. Cable, computers, cellular phones . . . it can all get a bit confusing. So when Pastor Stevens complained to his new secretary that he didn't think that the paging device folks asked him to wear was working, she was gentle in pointing out that he was wearing his garage door opener. That of course explained why his pager wasn't having much success opening the garage door.

Pastor Stevens had all the tools. He just needed a little good information on how to use them. Today the body of Christ (the church) is facing a similar information crisis when it comes to spiritual gifts. God has given us everything we need to grow to maturity, but in some cases we just can't seem to get the tools working correctly. In many local fellowships the gifts of the Spirit are either overlooked or misused. Those gifts that were given to create unity sometimes create dissension or frustration. A little good information would go a long way toward getting us to operate at our divine potential.

Some people fail to use their spiritual gifts because they simply don't know they have any. Since they've never been compelled to jump up to the pulpit and preach like John the Baptist, they think that when God passed out spiritual gifts they must have been behind the door. Others mistakenly believe that gifts are reserved for the superspiritual or the "professional Christian," those in full-time service. But Paul makes it clear that "to each one the manifestation of the Spirit is given" (1 Corinthians 12:7). Incidentally, this means that every Christian has been given the Spirit of God. If the Spirit manifests Himself through "each one," the Spirit must indwell "each one." We all have gifts, but if we're in the dark as to how to find them, they are of very little use.

I once heard a story of a man who had too much to drink. He stumbled around under a streetlight, obviously searching for something, when an onlooker asked if he could be of help. The drunk said, "Yes, I'm looking for my car keys."

"Well, where do you last remember seeing them," said the would-be good Samaritan.

"Over by that car," replied the drunk.

Puzzled, the passerby asked, "Why are you looking over here."

The man answered, "Because the light's better over here."

While searching for their spiritual gifts, many sincere followers of Christ are looking in the wrong place.

Unfortunately, they're looking for their gifts through an *inward* experience. If you're serious about *finding* and *using* your gifts, you must always look for an outward opportunity. Here's why. The Greek word for gifts of the Spirit literally means "grace gift." God is giving grace to the body of Christ in order to make us "mature." Now, here's the catch: the grace that is coming to you is intended to be given to others. In a sense, you are just the mailman. That's why Paul says, "the manifestation of the Spirit is given," not for you alone, but "for the common good" (1 Corinthians 12:7), "that the body of Christ may be built up" (Ephesians 4:12). So if you want to find your gift, look to the needs of God's people, not inward for a selfish experience. If you ask yourself, "Where are people hurting," the answer that tugs at your heart will guide you to your gift.

In my travels throughout the world, I've seen hundreds who know they have been given certain gifts, but because of pride or peer pressure they want to trade them in for gifts that seem more "glamorous." Regretfully, these people are unaware of their place in the body of Christ. They haven't figured out what the Christian weatherman knew. When thanked for bringing such a beautiful spring day, he quickly remarked, "Don't thank me, I'm not in management; I'm just in sales." No Christian is in management, especially when it comes to equipping the church for service. God says He gives gifts "to each one, just as He determines." Selecting your spiritual gifts is a sovereign act of God. Your job is to use them making sales for Christ's kingdom.

There is a great deal of needless confusion surrounding the use of spiritual gifts. Every Christmas I become a living example of why. I receive or purchase gifts that require assembly. The first thing I do is open the box and tear into the job like a tornado. On most occasions I end up with a few mysterious parts left over. That sends me searching through the trash for the instruction book! I wish one year I could just wise up and read the manual first. The Bible says a great deal about finding and using your spiritual gifts. Now, if we could just get folks to follow the instructions, we would all be a lot better off.

JUST DO IT

READ 1 CORINTHIANS 12–14. Make a list of the dos and don'ts in finding and using spiritual gifts.

21
LIVING LETTERS

You show that you are a letter from Christ, the result of our ministry, written not with ink but with the Spirit of the living God, not on tablets of stone but on tablets of human hearts.

2 CORINTHIANS 3:3

DURING THE KOREAN WAR A SMALL GROUP of believers were huddled in a chapel when communist soldiers broke in. One of the soldiers pulled a portrait of Christ off the wall, lined every one up, and at gunpoint ordered the group to spit on the picture and curse Christ. The first three men in line were leaders of the church. Each of them did as they were instructed. Next came a little girl who fell upon the portrait and wiped away the spit with her skirt. She then looked up and said, "Go ahead and kill me. I cannot curse His name." The soldiers then blindfolded the four and took them out behind the church. With three bullets they killed the men, but let the girl go free. Even these hardened communists were moved by her devotion to Christ.

The testimony of a Christian life is one of the most potent weapons we have in conquering our world for Christ. Our words are certainly important, but they have no power unless our lives shout that our words are true. "Let your light shine before men." Jesus said, "that they may see your good deeds and praise your Father in heaven" (Matthew 5:16).

During the rule of the vicious Roman emperor Nero, a special group of soldiers was recruited out of the amphitheater. They were trained and sent to fight the barbarians in Gaul. Nero was very suspicious of growing rebellion. When he heard that many of his soldiers had become loyal to Jesus, he sent orders that all Christian soldiers should be put to death.

When word reached a centurion named Vespian, he called his men together and ordered all who claimed Christ as king to step forward. Forty men did. Vespian pleaded with each of the men to renounce their allegiance to Christ, but not one would. Not willing to raise his sword against his own men, Vespian ordered the forty to be stripped naked and marched onto a nearby frozen lake. Vespian listened to the men as they sang and chanted through the long cold night, but as the hours passed the singing faded. Near dawn Vespian watched as one poor soul crawled in from the ice and up to his fire. Overwhelmed at the dedication of the thirty-nine who stayed in the snow, Vespian took off his clothes and took the place of the one. He died there with the thirty-nine.

Even the most eloquent words are impotent if your lifestyle denies them. But nothing delivers the truth of the gospel with more impact and conviction than a Christian who walks what he talks. Peter knew from his own experience the difficulty of harmonizing talk with walk, but he also knew the powerful impact of a living testimony. He encourages us to "Live such good lives among the pagans that, though they accuse you of doing wrong, they may see your good deeds and glorify God on the day he visits us" (1 Peter 2:12).

Some will be joining us in heaven because of what they have heard, but most will be there because of what they have seen.

JUST DO IT

HERE ARE a list of words that may bring to mind areas where your living letter could use a little polish. Think through them slowly and ask the Lord if there needs to be some adjustment:

- temper
- entertainment
- promises
- tongue
- habits
- places

22
HEALING THE FROG

"I tell you the truth, if you have faith as small as a mustard seed, you can say to this mountain, 'Move from here to there' and it will move. Nothing will be impossible for you."

MATTHEW 17:20

I T WAS 1979 AND THE PHONE didn't ring that often for DeGarmo and Key. To our shock and amazement, someone all the way on the other side of the country called requesting our high-energy ministerial services. We were delighted to answer.

In those days, both equipment and band traveled in a well-used seven-year-old Chevrolet truck. It was affectionately called "the Frog," because with the weight of the band and all our equipment the front end of the truck pointed skyward as if at any minute it would attempt to leap.

The trip was more than two thousand miles from Memphis to San Francisco. For the most part it was straight down Interstate 40 until you saw the Pacific. We pretended not to notice we had no air conditioning, even though it was July and we were traveling through the desert. All seemed to be going quite well until Kenny, our bass player, pointed out the black smoke (that always seemed to follow us) was getting thicker and blacker. Eventually the smoking was accompanied by an ominous, rhythmic clicking and thumping from under the hood.

Quickly checking the road map, Eddie decided we should try to limp into Needles, California, for repair. We pulled over to the first garage we came to, but they couldn't even look at it that day or the next. Checking the phone book, we found a shop, thankfully, just down the street. (Of course, everything is "just down the street" in Needles.)

We were advised to make ourselves comfortable. After several hours of banging and twisting, the mechanic offered us his diagnosis. It wasn't good. We had three burnt thingamabobs requiring a couple of chrome dexters and a dual malvo . . . or something like that. The long and short of it was the Frog wouldn't roll for two days.

We, of course, argued that this was totally unacceptable because San Francisco desperately needed our help. Mike, the mechanic, pointed out that nothing short of a miracle would get our truck back on the road. Mike's choice of words was providential. After a brief huddle that involved a pretty strange theological discussion, we decided to raise the hood and prayerfully lay hands on our sick engine.

I'd give a hundred dollars for a picture of those two tobacco-chewing mechanics when they saw us begin to pray with our hands outstretched on the radiator of that old Chevy. After praying, we thanked them both, hopped back in and headed for the interstate. The older of the two objected, swearing that we wouldn't get it off the lot. Smiling, we cranked the Frog up and waved good-bye.

Laughing at first, the old man followed us in his wrecker. After fifty miles we saw him make a U-turn and head back to Needles. We continued driving all night, arriving at our concert location just in time to set up and play. Oh yeah, the truck motor did finally give out. It went kerplunk just as we turned into the parking lot. We coasted up to the loading door. The San Francisco mechanic that repaired it said the motor had fused into a solid ball of metal. The saints there took up an offering and we bought the Frog a new motor for the trip home.

You know, some folks look at life from a horizontal point of view. Like the guy from Missouri (the Show-me State), they have to see it in order to believe it. Other folks look at the world vertically. They see it because they believe it. These are the kind of people who pray for the sick and lay hands on truck motors. The horizontal crowd spends their days broken down somewhere in a rational desert . . . and the vertical crowd waves farewell as they cross the horizon, leaving miracles in their wake.

JUST DO IT

CALL OR (better yet) visit someone in your church who needs prayer. Pray with them out loud so there will be no doubt about what you are asking God to do. Don't worry, God can handle it.

23
PITY PARTIES

Whom have I in heaven but you? And earth has nothing I desire besides you. My flesh and my heart may fail, but God is the strength of my heart and my portion forever.

PSALM 73:25–26

DAVID WAS AN AMAZING GUY. He often soared spiritually higher than any of us ever will, but at other times he sank into the familiar grip of despair. Psalm 73 gives us a view of both. At one moment, David is possessed by jealousy and frustration; the next, he is filled with exhilaration. The question that brings David into the clutches of gloom is one that many of us ask in those moments when we feel alone or defeated. Why do the wicked prosper?

Indirectly this question challenges God's wisdom, power, or virtue. Just beneath the surface, David is saying, "God, are you unaware that good things are happening to bad people, or is it that you are unwilling or unable to prevent it?" David is experiencing what one child typically feels when another receives a gift while she is overlooked. David is having what we call in our home a pity party.

As a teenager, David was able to face and kill Goliath while the other warriors of Israel looked on in fear. To his credit, he looked at Goliath through the lens of faith that makes all sizes relative to God's. The soldiers viewed Goliath through human reason. Next to the men of Israel, he looked huge. Next to God, Goliath looked tiny. The Israelite soldiers thought Goliath was far too big to hit. David saw him as too big to miss. The soldiers felt that the bigger the warrior was, the harder he would be to fell. From David's point of view, the bigger he was, the harder he would fall.

David's point of view was from a hill called "divine viewpoint." Standing on this hill, a man could see God was in charge; therefore, the victory was certain.

Somewhere between the slaying of Goliath and the pity party of Psalm 73, David nearly stumbled into the deep pit of envy. "But as for me, my feet had almost slipped; I had nearly lost my foothold. For I envied the arrogant when I saw the prosperity of the wicked. They have no struggles; their bodies are healthy and strong. They are free from the burdens common to man" (verses 2–5).

Suddenly, David was far from that hilltop. He was now looking at the world from the pit of self-pity. "I have kept my heart pure; in vain have I washed my hands in innocence" (verse 13). David's misplaced sorrow was based on two very difficult-to-admit truths and one very false assumption. The first truth is that sin is fun, at least temporarily. Sin is enjoyable and can bring short-term pleasure. That is why we find it so difficult to pass up. If sin immediately brought pain like that of picking up a hot pan without a potholder, there would be a lot more righteous people in the world. But sin can be fun and that's why it is so tempting.

Second, sin is hard to ignore. We are never safe from its lure or out of its reach. No monastery can protect us from sin. Its strategic base of operation is deep in our hearts. Therefore, holiness is a constant, day-to-day struggle to silence the inner voice that offers us temporary pleasure at the expense of eternal joy.

Now, as to David's false assumption, he assumed that the reward for holiness was prosperity and/or happiness. The truth is, our reward for obedience is neither.

Holy people are rarely rich. As Paul pointed out to the Corinthians, "not many [of you] were of noble birth" (1 Corinthians 1:26). In fact, many times righteous behavior is the cause of poverty. The world hated Jesus, and if you love Him the world will hate you as well.

Second, happiness is never ever promised as a reward for following Jesus. Happiness is dependent upon happenstance. If good circumstances come, I'm happy; if bad things come, I'm sad. Joy and peace are our reward for obedience, and they are far less fragile than happiness. Joy and peace come as a result of being in the presence of Christ. Where He is, there is joy. Even if we are led into the eye of the hurricane, if Jesus goes before us, we have peace in the midst of the wind and the waves. If we follow Peter to prison, we can still fill the air with the sounds of "Amazing Grace."

Happiness is not the reward for holiness, and hard times are not the reward for sin. The three so-called friends of Job shared David's humanistic view of the relationship between sin and pain. They assumed that the reason for Job's plight was some unconfessed sin. In the same way, the injured man in the story of the good Samaritan was passed by because it was assumed that he was robbed and beaten in retribution for his own sin. But pain does not come into the Christian's life to punish; it comes to glorify God and to make us better servants. Jesus tells us in the case of Lazarus that some things happen so that God will be glorified. Paul teaches us that even when bad things do come our way, God means them for our good (Romans 8:28–29).

David's pity party comes to a sudden conclusion in the sanctuary of God. David enters God's presence and sees from his knees what he was unable to see from his own kingly throne. He sees the essence of the divine point of view that is the panorama of final destiny. The believer is guaranteed victory in the end, and those who mock the word of God are promised damnation. "Those who are far from you will perish; you destroy all who are unfaithful to you. But as for me, it is good to be near God. I have made the Sovereign LORD my refuge" (Psalm 73:27–28).

In the end, the reward believers receive for holiness is one the wicked will always consider garbage. Yet to the believer, our reward is more precious than gold. We will have Jesus, the eternal fountain of our joy and peace. To drink deeply and eternally from these waters infinitely overshadows the small sacrifices on our journey to them.

Why do the wicked prosper? Well, that depends on how you define prosperity. If you are one of those who are learning daily to let go of this temporary world in order to grasp eternal righteousness, you might say the wicked don't prosper. For what real gain is it to chase after things that will rust, fade, or die . . . and then pay the bill for them eternally with your soul.

JUST DO IT

LIST THOSE things that will follow you into eternity. Here's a hint—memories, relationships, etc. Spend your prayer time giving thanks for all those things in your life that can't be taken away. Next time you have a moment to venture off the beaten path, take a cruise through a part of town that will remind you of your blessings.

24
A CHECKLIST FOR DECISIONS

*I run in the path of your commands, for you have
set my heart free.*

PSALM 119:32

MY FATHER TRIED WITH SOME DEGREE of success to teach me that
if you want to get a job done, you need to have the right tool and
the know-how to use it. I have tried to pass this philosophy onto
my wife and children. I went out for the weekend to speak at a
Canadian Bible college. Before leaving town on Thursday, Anita
reminded me of one of those little chores that husbands are sup-
posed to take care of. Our toilet was stopped up.

I headed toward the local hardware store. When I walked
into the plumbing department, I immediately recognized the right
tool for the job. It was the T-35 Super Handy Man plunger. My
Super Handy Man plunger did a great job. I departed for Canada
feeling like my dad would be proud.

When I returned just before dawn on Monday morning, I
noticed that my Super Handy Man plunger was sitting on the floor
next to the head of our bed. I was a bit more than curious. I
wanted to wait till breakfast for an explanation, but I just couldn't
imagine what use Anita might have had for my new plunger next
to the bed.

I whispered, "Honey, I notice you've been using my Super
Handy Man plunger."

Still half-asleep, she said, "I heard noises in the attic, and I
thought it might have been a burglar."

I said, "Sweetheart, the plunger is big, black, and scary look-ing, but it's rubber. Were you planning to suck their faces off?"

Anita had the right general idea, just the wrong tool. We have mace for burglars, but my Super Handy Man plunger is for those manly jobs. Our burglars were in fact squirrels. Acorns would have served as better tools than plungers.

God has given you and me the tools we need to make it through. In fact He has given us the whole toolbox, His Word. The Bible doesn't contain *every* answer to *every* question you may have, but it does give the guidance needed to see you through *every* situation that may arise.

There are some who see little use for the Bible today—even those who call themselves Christians. Some feel it's out of date for the complex decisions of our times. They prefer to rely on common sense and personal experience to guide them. But these two seeing-eye dogs—common sense and personal experience—may lead you into oncoming traffic. Neither of them can see the eighteen-wheelers barreling through the spiritual dimension. Good common sense can, in fact, be dangerous. My Grandmother Pearl used to point this out. She tirelessly quoted this Scripture hoping the repe-tition would penetrate the thick skull of a rebellious teenager: "There is a way that seems right to a man, but in the end it leads to death" (Proverbs 16:25).

What I struggled to grasp was that just because I thought I was doing the right thing, didn't necessarily ensure I wouldn't crash. The men in this verse from Proverbs weren't doing what they *knew* was wrong. They sincerely thought that they were right, yet they still ended up dying. They probably went to hell saying, "I'm sure God knows I meant well." Yet meaning well had *zero* impact in preventing their destruction. Good intentions and right behavior can be separated by an eternity of distance. It is impos-sible for us to find the right path without divine aid.

We are born with our moral compass set in the wrong direc-tion. That's why it has to be recalibrated with God's Word before it can be trusted to lead. When you think about it, isn't it rather pompous to think your intelligence and experience in any way compare to that of the intelligence that spoke the worlds into existence and the wisdom that comes from living from eternity past. If you think you have better decision-making skills than God, you've got squirrels in your attic, too!

Here's a checklist of scriptural tools that I often use for making a decision:

_____ 1. Does it line up with direct statements and principles in the Bible? There are some things in the Bible that you just don't need to pray about because God isn't going to change His mind. For instance, you don't ever need to pray about getting drunk. The Bible is direct on this matter.

When it comes to principles of Scripture, decision-making may take a little more thought, but it doesn't require a rocket scientist. For instance, the Bible says, don't marry an unbeliever. "Do not be yoked together with unbelievers. For what do righteousness and wickedness have in common? Or what fellowship can light have with darkness?" (2 Corinthians 6:14). So you don't need to pray about whether or not to date one. Dating is the prelude to marriage, and if your affection is set on a non-Christian, then your obligation is to pray and witness to him or her, but not to date.

_____ 2. Do those in leadership around you feel strongly one way or the other? God has made us part of a body. That interdependency gives us a safety net. He has given someone somewhere the responsibility of watching over you. These pastors, youth leaders, parents, etc. will probably know more of God's Word and have experience in applying it. "For lack of guidance a nation falls, but many advisers make victory sure" (Proverbs 11:14).

_____ 3. Have you quietly consulted your heart. God has sent us the ultimate counselor, His Spirit. He brings both conviction and peace. Colossians 3:15 says, "Let the peace of Christ rule in your hearts." The

Greek language indicates that peace serves like a referee at a sporting event. He says nothing until you've broken a rule or gotten out of bounds. The peace of Christ works in similar fashion. You may not realize you have it until God blows the whistle on your behavior and that peace is gone.

Discerning peace involves a side of prayer that is often neglected. Prayer is about asking and listening. He already knows what your will is. Take time to quietly listen to His.

_____ 4. Make a move. There is a story about a man who bowed one morning to pray, but his prayer was interrupted by an emergency radio broadcast. The announcer warned that a flood was coming, move to higher ground. The praying man resumed his prayer asking, "Lord, should I flee?" Soon it began to rain and as the water entered his home, a man's voice called out from a passing boat, "Come on, jump in." Again the man prayed. "Lord, should I leave?" but he heard nothing. Finally the man was forced by the raging water to the rooftop where he was spotted by a helicopter. But again, having prayed and received no answer, the man stayed only to be swept away and drowned. Standing before God's throne in heaven, the man said, "Lord, don't get me wrong, I'm really glad to be here, but why didn't you answer my prayer?" God replied, "What do you mean, my son? I sent you a radio broadcast, a boat, and a helicopter."

It is easier to steer a moving car than a parked one. Get off the dime. God is capable of getting you to the right destination.

JUST DO IT

YOU JUST read the checklist. Use it!

25
THE LAST SAFE PLACE

Let us not give up meeting together, as some are in
the habit of doing, but let us encourage one another—
and all the more as you see the Day approaching.
HEBREWS 10:25

ONE OF THE MOST IMPORTANT WAYS God speaks to us today is through the voice of the local church. The folks who grace the halls of those community gatherings may not radiate like Moses when he came down from the mountain, but they bring us the Word of God and a whole lot more. When I hear someone say, "I'm close to God but I don't like going to church," I know that I'm hearing the voice of a Lone Ranger who will soon be ambushed by the wolves of sin. No church is perfect, but for the Christian it's the place to be. Here are four good reasons why.

First, it's not a good suggestion. It's an order. The author of Hebrews tells us "not to give up meeting together, as some are in the habit of doing" (10:25). We could stop here. This verse should be enough. (But I won't.)

Second, the church has been promised divine protection from that hungry lion that prowls the earth looking for some poor sap to devour. When Jesus asked Peter, "Who do you say I am?" Peter went to the head of the class by saying, "You are the Christ, the Son of the living God." Jesus then made a remarkable promise. He told Peter this was a revelation that had come to him from God. Then He made this promise, "On this rock I will build my church, and the gates of Hades will not overcome it" (Matthew 16:18). Are you looking for a place that is guaranteed success in the fight against the forces of darkness? It's just down the street.

When Paul recommended that a certain unrepentant man be turned over to Satan for the destruction of the flesh, what he was saying was "no longer permit this man to enjoy the protection from Satan that has been given to us." The church is a safe haven from the powers of darkness.

Third, church is a place where you can find and use your spiritual gift. First Corinthians 12:7 tells us who has gifts of the Spirit and why they are given. Paul says, "to each one the manifestation of the Spirit is given." Who has gifts of the Spirit? "Each of us." And why are they given? "For the common good."

That should lead us to ask, "Whose common good?" Paul tells us it's for the "body of Christ." The church operates like a human body. Though "the body is a unit . . . it is made up of many parts." If we were intended to be the hand or voice in that body, but we have been self-amputated by an unwillingness to get involved, the local body of Christ is wounded and incomplete. Not only may you never learn your gift, but others will never benefit from it.

When I am asked, "How do you get into Christian music?" I say, "Join the choir." Are you the next Billy Graham? Teach Sunday School. Maybe you don't sing or speak well. You can mow grass, drive the elderly, help with accounting, sweep a floor, pass out songbooks. You get the idea.

The church is not a building, it's people committed to each other's physical and spiritual needs. You've been given a gift by God that was intended to help us and we need it now!

Finally, the best reason to be in church is because church is where Jesus is. "For where two or three come together in my name, there am I with them" (Matthew 18:20). This isn't to say Jesus is not with individuals as well, but it does suggest that in some unique way His presence is manifested when Christians gather as a group. If you want the full experience of being in His presence, you'll have to do it with the others in the family of God.

The bottom line: God has told us to be a part of a local church. He's promised to protect us there. It's where you were intended to serve and be served. And that's where Jesus is. So I'll see you at church on Sunday.

JUST DO IT

IF YOU miss church this week, will anybody notice? Get involved with your church.

26

To Catch a Thief

The man who does not enter the sheep pen by the gate, but climbs in by some other way, is a thief and a robber.

JOHN 10:1

YOU'VE HEARD IT SAID THAT CRIME is no laughing matter. For the most part that's true, but on some occasions it can be downright funny. Take for instance a case reported to the Los Angeles Police Department dubbed the "Poop Snatcher." Mrs. Hollis Sharpe took Jonathan, her miniature poodle, out every evening to do his business. Since Mrs. Sharpe was a thoughtful neighbor, she took a scoop and a plastic bag along to collect the evidence. On the night of November 14, Jonathan had finished and Mrs. Sharpe was walking home with the bag in her right hand, when a mugger attacked from behind, grabbing the "spoils" and speeding away in a car. I'd have paid a high price for a ticket to see the look on his face when he checked out the loot.

Charles Meriweather broke into the home of a thirty-four-year-old Baltimore woman. When he discovered that the woman only had $11.50 in cash, he demanded that she write him a check. "Who shall I make it out to?" she said. The thief replied, "Charles Meriweather," adding, "and it better not bounce or I'll be back." Meriweather was arrested hours after that.

Not all thieves are as dumb as these guys were or as easy to point out. John 10 speaks of a variety of religious thieves who are hideously clever. They dress like shepherds, and every theft is an inside job. Jesus warns that these shepherds have "illegally" entered the sheep pen. Their mission is "to steal and kill and destroy" (John 10:10). False shepherds were in business in Jesus' day, and they are still working in the sheep pen at present.

Last Easter a prominent Memphis pastor said these words from his pulpit: "Jesus being the most innocent person who ever lived did not deserve to be put to death in any fashion, especially crucifixion. God did not in any way will Jesus to be put to death. What then should we say that God wanted regarding Jesus' death? We should say that God willed Jesus be an honest, well-balanced, truthful human being: a role model for humanity. . . . God was willing to allow His Son to be made to suffer and to be put to death for the purpose of teaching us how to cope with suffering."

There have been volumes written about cults, false doctrines, and how to spot them. They are interesting, but perhaps unnecessary. A Christian needs to extract the answer to only two questions in order to tell the wolves from the sheep. True believers answer these questions differently from every other religion in the world:

1. Who was Jesus?

2. Why did He die?

Only His sheep know Jesus as the one and only God of the universe, and only His sheep believe He is the "lamb slain from before the foundations of the world," sent to die for our sin. All other discussions are just little planets orbiting the eternal Son. To visit them can sometimes distract from these two all-important questions.

As for the Easter sermon, this impostor pastor completely missed the importance of Christ's death. Certainly, it can be said that Jesus was a wonderful role model, but to say that His death was nothing more is a dagger in the heart of the gospel. Jesus died as a substitute for our sin, and this concrete-and-steel truth is the only bridge over the chasm of death and hell.

What's truly sad is that this flock listened, whispered amen, said a prayer, and went home feeling blessed. They didn't realize they'd been fleeced by an impostor posing as a shepherd. They didn't know every eloquent word contained just enough truth to disguise it from a lie, but not enough truth to get the sheep to heaven. They listened without objection because they didn't know God's Word.

To catch a thief we must be able to spot them. We must study God's Word each day with a passion that demonstrates our lives depend on it. We might one day find ourselves in a situation where it may. Jesus promises that man lives "on every word that comes from the mouth of God," and he is just as certain to die with out it.

JUST DO IT

JOIN OR start a Bible study group. Or check into attending one semester of Bible classes at your local Christian college.

27

THE BATTLE FOR THE BIBLE

For the word of God is living and active. Sharper than any double-edged sword, it penetrates even to dividing soul and spirit.

HEBREWS 4:12

A WELL-KNOWN CHRISTIAN ACTIVIST once said, "If someone on American television in 1959 said I've had a vision: In the next thirty years we will have murdered twenty-five million children in ways too barbaric to describe [abortion]. Sodomites will be parading in the streets. Politicians will be proclaiming gay pride week. Your tax money will be going to fund blasphemy and homosexual pornography. It will be illegal for a public schoolteacher to recite the Lord's prayer or read Psalm 23 in her classroom, but that same teacher will be able to tell your child where to get a condom or an abortion without your consent or knowledge; that there would be a drug crisis, that we would have mass crime going on in our country. Who would have believed it? Nobody." He's right, America has changed.

We are going down like the giant *Titanic,* sinking morally into a cesspool of our own making. Some point to economic factors, blaming our social ills on poverty. Yet the percentage of Americans below the poverty line is roughly the same now as it was thirty years ago.

Others point to the assault on the family, citing the soaring divorce rate and the rise in illegitimate births, yet long before the fabric that keeps American families together started to unravel, it was our collapsing moral foundation that permitted this free fall.

From America's very beginning the Bible has been the mortar that has held the foundation together. After reading Isaiah 40:22—"He sits enthroned above the circle of the earth"—Columbus was convinced he could sail around the world. The pilgrims in search of the freedom to live according to the Bible left their homelands. The Founding Fathers referred to the Bible often in creating our system of government. But in recent times, attacks on God's Word have removed its influence from American culture. As the Bible has disappeared, crime and moral decay have filled the spiritual vacuum.

The challenge of God's words goes all the way back to the garden of Eden. In Genesis 3, the serpent used two tactics to tempt Eve that are in common use to this very day: doubt and denial. First, he attempted to cast doubt on God's words by saying to Eve, "Did God really say you must not eat of this tree?" Then he directly denied God's Word saying, "You will not surely die."

Thousands of years later, Jesus warned His disciples that God's Word is still the focus of Satan's attack. In the parable of the sower (Matthew 13:18–23), He tells them that the seed that goes out is "the word" and if it doesn't take root "the evil one" comes to snatch it away. In other words, Satan is in the business of uprooting both the convicting and comforting influence of God's Word.

Today in America we are witnessing the legacy of a more recent assault on the Bible that started a little more than a hundred years ago. In 1859, Charles Darwin took a shot at the first chapter of the Bible with the release of his book, *On the Origin of Species*. In spite of the fact that there was (and is) no scientific proof that one species can evolve into another, by 1930 the non-Christian science and educational community largely accepted Darwin's theory as fact. By the mid-1960s, evolution had replaced creation science in high schools and colleges. That was the first domino.

The second one was predictable. With many Americans now doubting the trustworthy nature of the Bible, Madalyn Murray O'Hair sued successfully to remove Bible reading and prayer from public schools.

The results of the new moral-free education curriculums have been devastating. Who could have dreamed of an America that needed on-campus policemen and metal detectors where children commit murder for a pair of tennis shoes? I do not believe it's a coincidence that these things seemed to arrive the day we started firing principals for praying and teachers for carrying Bibles.

How the forces of darkness hate God's Word.

This two-edged sword convicts with such impact that sometimes just the sight of it can penetrate a sin-numbed heart. One night a friend asked me to go out to play a brand-new video game. The problem was that the only place in town that had this game was a restaurant near the university. I wasn't so sure that was an appropriate place for a Christian to be. My practice is that any place I feel comfortable carrying my Bible into is usually OK (I said usually). I told my pal if we could take our Bibles, I was game. The most amazing thing happened that night. People kept interrupting our video game saying things like "I used to go to church," or "I'm really a Christian, I've just been wandering a bit lately." Sometimes just seeing the Bible has the power to convict of sin.

If America is able to turn around, it will not come because of a political movement; it will come as the result of a Bible movement. God's holy Word is the only convicting power strong enough to undo the stranglehold of sin. Christians must dedicate themselves to carrying it in both their hearts and their hands. Apart from God's Word we are helpless to save our nation from moral implosion. It is clear that the battle for the Bible is now the battle for America.

JUST DO IT

MAKE A commitment to read a chapter of the Bible each day with a friend at work or school.

28
Garbage In, Garbage Out

Do not conform any longer to the pattern of this world, but be transformed by the renewing of your mind. Then you will be able to test and approve what God's will is—his good, pleasing and perfect will.

ROMANS 12:2

THE APOSTLE PAUL SAYS THAT IF WE want to know God's will, we must "renew" our minds. Now there are two ongoing jobs for the Christian who desires a new mind. He has to put the good stuff in and keep the bad stuff out.

Putting the good stuff in is not all that difficult. What it amounts to is forming good habits, like reading your Bible or watching the Family Channel. Keeping the bad stuff out is a little more of a challenge in the information age, and the reason comes down to simple biology.

The brain works like a supercomputer. It is constantly scanning with its eyes and ears, recording and storing gigabites of information the world around sends our way. The problem is you can't turn it off.

I'm a sports nut. I'll be watching the Orlando Magic play, and when halftime comes I make a fast break for the refrigerator. While hastily preparing something I can slam dunk, I'll catch myself singing, "We build excitement . . . Pontiac." One night it occurred to me that I didn't like that song. I didn't want it in my brain, but I couldn't do anything about it. I was doomed to sing it the rest of the night. Once it's there, it's there. You can't unring a noisy bell. You can just wait and hope the sound fades away quickly.

Now Pontiac doesn't think that I'm going to throw down my sandwich and head to the closest Pontiac dealer the moment the commercial is over. They just want me to remember Pontiac the next time I'm shopping for a car. Some folks in the academic world will tell you that what you see and hear doesn't affect behavior, but the people who pay a million dollars a minute for Super Bowl advertising time would disagree. They believe this little Sunday School axiom:

Sow a thought, reap a deed.
Sow a deed, reap a habit.
Sow a habit, reap a lifestyle.
Sow a lifestyle, reap a destiny.

Advertisers want you to make *their* products *your* lifestyle. So often they are successful because the only way to keep their sales pitches out of our hearts is to keep away from the information, and that is nearly impossible.

Our hearts absorb the ambiance of our environment, and it affects us for good or evil. When Lot moved to the Plains of Jordan, he was attracted by the "well-watered land" (Genesis 13:10). Five chapters later, the angels that came to destroy Sodom had to physically force him to leave. Lot's attractions had changed. It wasn't the "well-watered land," it was sinful Sodom he longed for. It first began when Lot chose to move near Sodom. The next time we see Lot he lives in Sodom, and, what's worse, Sodom lives in him. The constant exposure to sin turned Lot from a prosperous man of God to a penniless drunk hiding in a cave.

If you are constantly seeing and hearing sinful things, it will eventually come back to you in sinful behavior. The Bible commands us to "*resist*" the devil (1 Peter 5:9) but not the temptations of "the flesh." Paul instructs us to "*flee* the evil desires of youth" (2 Timothy 2:22). The principle of fleeing the flesh as opposed to resisting it is about getting physically away from exposure to temptation. The idea is exactly what Joseph did when sexually tempted by Potiphar's wife (Genesis 39:11). He ran and so should we when we are exposed to the presence of those things that stimulate us to sin. You can't move to a monastery, but at the least you can control the environment of your own home. Guard your heart. It's far easier to prevent garbage from getting in than it is to get it out.

JUST DO IT

Is IT time to cut the cable or maybe television in general? Is it time for a review of your music collection? Is there a place or friend that you need to avoid? Come on, just do it.

29
PAINTING WITH ONE COLOR

It was he who gave some to be apostles, some to be prophets, some to be evangelists and some to be pastors and teachers . . . so that the body of Christ may be built up until we all reach unity in the faith.

EPHESIANS 4:11–13

NOT LONG AGO A BIG BROUHAHA came up that pitted a military academy's policy against women's rights. Shannon Faulkner convinced a federal judge to force the all-male Citadel Academy to admit her. Once in, Faulkner refused to substitute her more-than-shoulder-length locks for the traditional "knob cut." You might be tempted to side with Faulkner until you hear the military's side of the story. According to a spokesperson, "The buzz cut is an important part of diminishing the differences between individuals. It helps our people more quickly lose their personal identity and become a team." Uniform haircuts are intended to have the same effect as uniform clothes. From the military's point of view, the more alike in appearance, the better. The school's attorneys argued that the right to enforce a uniform appearance was a vital tool in creating team spirit. Maybe they are right, uniformity doesn't guarantee unity of purpose, but it may be one of the only tools at the disposal of the armed services.

According to the Bible, diversity is the tool that God uses to bring us together in unity. He gives us all different gifts of the Spirit that force us to become interdependent. Some are teachers, some are administrators, some have the gift of helps, and so on. But all are given a gift, and no one but Christ possesses all the gifts. The isolated Christian is the spiritually deprived and impoverished Christian. Likewise those who desire to have all the grace of God available in Christ must learn to celebrate our differences.

Even with the varied gifts of the Spirit, achieving unity is no piece of cake. Uniformity is much more in tune with our fallen nature and is thus easier to achieve.

Unity in purpose is something that begins in the heart, while uniformity of appearance is totally external. Unity of purpose requires trust, while uniformity of personality comes from fear and mistrust. People by nature gravitate to those who look, act, and think like themselves. That's why the most segregated hour of the week in every American city is between eleven and twelve o'clock on Sunday morning. The human longing for uniformity contributes to the divisions in the body of Christ we call denominations. One church is the Teaching Church, another is a Praise Church, and so on. Churches, like cities, do take on unique personalities, but they injure the body of Christ when they celebrate one gift to the exclusion of the others.

Using Paul's body analogy, one group makes welcome the "feet" of Christ's body while another building is filled with "hands." If the body of Christ were a football team, one group would have only linemen, another only quarterbacks. Even a nonathlete knows a pro football team of all quarterbacks—even if they were Joe Montanas and John Elways—would still be destined to lose.

From a personal point of view, consider the fact that you and I forfeit a measure of the grace of God when we prefer uniformity to diversity. Diversity puts us around people with a variety of grace, yielding gifts that are given to help us grow into the mature image of Christ.

In a larger sense, think of how much clearer the world would see Christ if the body worked together. Painting with one color, even if it is our favorite color, will never create the beautiful mosaic of Christ that the entire church is intended to be.

JUST DO IT

LIST WHAT you think might be the spiritual strength of each of the denominations that you are familiar with. Ask God to help you see the value of Christians different from you. If it makes sense for you, with the permission of your pastor and/or parents, arrange with some friends to make a Sunday night "field trip" to a church that is predominately of a different race than yours.

30

"SIN-TRIFAGUL" FORCE

So I tell you this, and insist on it in the Lord, that you must no longer live as the Gentiles do, in the futility of their thinking. They are darkened in their understanding and separated from the life of God because of the ignorance that is in them due to the hardening of their hearts. Having lost all sensitivity, they have given themselves over to sensuality so as to indulge in every kind of impurity, with a continual lust for more.

EPHESIANS 4:17–19

IN THE CLASSIC *MERE CHRISTIANITY,* C. S. Lewis makes a profound observation concerning those little decisions of life. "Good and evil both grow at compound interest. That is why the little decisions you and I make every day are of such infinite importance. The smallest good act today is the capture of a strategic point from which, a few months later, you may be able to go onto victories you never dreamed of. An apparently trivial indulgence in lust or anger today is the loss of a ridge or railway line or bridgehead from which the enemy may launch an attack otherwise impossible."

Lewis rightly observes that it is in small decisions for right and wrong that we ultimately determine the larger outcome of our personal holiness. The journey to righteousness or damnation is filled in with millions of tiny footsteps, and no one ever gets to either outcome without first taking these little steps.

What Lewis describes with the skill of a surgeon's scalpel, Paul explains with the bluntness of a sledgehammer. In Ephesians 4:17–19, Paul describes the superhighway to hell taken by those who are said to be "darkened in their understanding and separate from the life of God." They are trapped in a vicious cycle of sin that follows this cyclical pattern:

1. hardening the heart

2. losing sensitivity

3. lusting for more

4. being darkened in understanding and further separated from God

It all begins by ignoring one of God's greatest gifts: the ability to blush. It has been said that man is the only creature who has the ability to blush, and he is the only creature that needs to. The end result of refusing to blush is losing that ability.

I know a fine Christian mother who at a darker time in her life had worked as an exotic dancer. Hearing her testimony gave me some insight into the transformation from Girl Scout to spiritual numbness. She said, "The first night I was terrified and ashamed. The next night my shame turned to embarrassment, and by the end of the week I felt nothing at all."

When I began playing guitar, the first obstacle to overcome was the excruciating pain. Pressing down the raised steel strings of an inexpensive instrument can be brutal on the sensitive fingers of a twelve-year-old. I would have never continued lessons had I not been assured that calluses would form and the pain would cease. I ignored the pain although my fingers bled. Eventually, the dead skin covered my shredded nerve endings and the pain stopped. Years of playing have killed all feeling in the fingertips of my left hand.

This is very similar to what takes place in the heart of one who is turning from God. Paul says, "Having lost all sensitivity, they have given themselves over to sensuality" (verse 19). They engage in sinfully stimulating behavior, but the problem is that because of the continuing loss of sensitivity, sin loses its thrill. Like the heroine addict, it requires increasingly higher doses of sin to achieve the same high. Thus they develop a continual lust for more. Perhaps this Scripture sheds light on the most horrible acts of men, such as sadomasochism and bondage. Becoming numb, sin addicts exhaust the ability of pleasure to stimulate, so they are forced to explore the world of pain.

When the cycle of sin comes back around for you and me, we find ourselves at a place where we first got on this superhighway. We feel the tug of lust along with the pang of conscious. Once again we are forced to make one of those seemingly small decisions. If we decide to turn that lust into a physical reality, we'll of course add thickness to the callous and further damage our conscience. Each time sin goes unresisted, the callous grows thicker and that tiny voice of warning grows fainter until one day there is no voice at all.

A tiny sin is like thread. Wrap it around me once, and I can easily break it. Wrap it around me twice, and still I can break it, but with more difficulty. Continue to wrap it around me unhindered, and the tiny thread may as well be a chain of steel. I lose my ability to break it at all.

The sin dealt with soonest is the sin dealt with easiest, while the voice of conscience is still loud and clear. It is essential to remember that where there is conviction there is still hope. The exotic-dancer-turned-godly-mother turned out to be a wonderful testimony of the power of God to break the cycle of sin and restore even a severely damaged conscience.

Now may be the time to put on your moral brakes and turn to a new direction before the "sin-trifagul force" of your actions propels you to a speed where the momentum of your life cannot be reversed.

JUST DO IT

IN EPHESIANS 4:25–32, Paul gives various examples of the sins that he is concerned with. Pray and pause through this list, stopping at each comma or period to allow the Holy Spirit to speak to you.

31
It Ain't Bragging . . .

Then Jesus said to her, "Your sins are forgiven."
The other guests began to say among themselves,
"Who is this who even forgives sins?"

LUKE 7:48

VEN THE FOOL SEEMS WISE WHEN he remains silent. It's those confounded little slips of the tongue that often give away our spiritual and intellectual bankruptcy. When a person says, "I've been a Christian my whole life," or "God helps those who help themselves," you have to suspect that Bible study isn't his or her strong suit. Another statement you may increasingly run into is, "I believe Jesus was the son of God, but I don't think He was really God Himself." This one seems to be cropping up more and more, especially on college campuses. It seems those intellectual types like to keep a politically correct, open mind even if they have to be wrong to do it.

Some "tender hearts" (with empty heads) abandon the deity of Christ searching for common ground with other of the world's religions. Still others prefer Christ the man to Christ our God because a smaller Jesus seems easier to ignore. Yet positions that make Christ just a fine man and noble teacher leave you with both feet planted firmly in midair. Even a casual Bible reader knows that Jesus' own words will not permit it . . . and neither will His deeds.

Take for instance what Jesus did for the repentant prostitute at Simon the Pharisee's house (Luke 7:38). She washed His feet with her tears and then dried them with her hair. Jesus then made this astonishing pronouncement, saying, "Your sins are forgiven."

Perhaps we're too familiar with statements like this, but most of us miss His incredible claim. How can anyone claim to forgive someone else's sins? This should be listed in the *Guinness Book of World Records* for the most incredibly stupid and egotistical thing ever said. This kind of blowhard conceit would totally deflate any claims of being humble and meek unless, of course, Jesus truly is God.

If you steal my guitar or throw a brick through my window, it is reasonable for me, under the right set of circumstances, to say, "I forgive you." After all, I was personally injured by your actions. In what way can Jesus tell this prostitute, no matter how sorry she is, that He forgives her? How has He been personally injured by her sin?

If Jesus is not God, then He has no right, much less the ability, to forgive anyone's sins, especially those that do not involve Him. Yet if Jesus really means it when He says, "I and the Father are one," then that's a different story.

As Jesus pronounced this lady of the night forgiven, the room erupted with the shocked onlookers saying, "Who is this man who even forgives sins?" The guests at Simon's dinner party understood that only God can forgive sins, and only God or a fool would claim to. Like the old pitcher Dizzy Dean would say, "It ain't bragging if you can do it."

JUST DO IT

SPEND YOUR prayer time confessing your sin to Jesus. Open your Bible to Galatians 5:17–24 and prayerfully read it. Pause at every comma to let God's Spirit speak to you about your sin.

32
WHEN BAD IS GOOD

And we know that in all things God works for the good of those who love him, who have been called according to his purpose. For those God foreknew he also predestined to be conformed to the likeness of his Son, that he might be the firstborn among many brothers.

ROMANS 8:28–29

ROMANS 8:28 TELLS US THAT GOD works in *all* things for our good, and sometimes this means using even our own mistakes.

In all the years I've known Jim, he's always been a play-it-by-the-book kind of a guy. So I was surprised to learn what an out-of-character thing he had done. He risked a military court-martial for a little fresh air and a couple hours of sleep.

In World War II, Jim was a marine on his way to the battle of Okinawa. Servicemen in transit had to sleep deep in the lower decks of their transport ships where it was always hot and noisy. Jim had a pal named Jorgensen, who was quite a character. Unlike Jim, he never played by the rules, and on this hot night I'm glad he didn't. Arguing that marines deserve a good night's rest before they go into battle, he persuaded Jim to sneak up to the top deck where they later fell asleep in a lifeboat. Sometime around dawn a kamikaze crashed into the lower deck of the ship causing a fiery explosion where Jim would have been sleeping had it not been for his pal Jorgensen. Jim, of course, wasn't there. He later went on to give his life to Christ, marry an Oklahoma girl named Jo, and become my dad.

God never approves of us doing what is wrong, but He has the ability to turn the worst of tragedies into good for those who love Him.

He's a bigger, more powerful God than some think. He doesn't just work some things together for our good. That would be too easy. He works "all things together for our good," even those tragedies that are of our own making. He's not the kind of God to thumb His nose and tell us, "You got what you deserved." Just the opposite. By His sovereign grace, He makes sure that we never get what we really deserve. (We deserve hell.)

Joseph, the son of Jacob, was an interesting character. When he grew up, he became one of the Bible's greatest heroes. Joseph had every reason to turn out just the opposite. You remember, his brothers sold him into slavery. Joseph was his father's favorite, and his brothers were so jealous that the Bible says they hated him (Genesis 37:4).

After falling from "favorite son" to "penniless slave," he suffered further indignity by being thrown into prison for refusing the advances of Potiphar's wife.

It was only after suffering years of disgrace that Joseph's mission started to come into focus. Because of his ability to interpret dreams, he was freed from prison and managed to become the second-most-powerful man in the known world.

Years later, Joseph's family fell on hard times, and the same brothers who had sold him into slavery stood before him begging for food and mercy. Joseph was no longer the little brother they had sold into slavery. He was a ruler with the power of life and death. Overcome by fear, his brothers cast themselves at Joseph's feet. If it had been a movie, the next thing you would have heard would have been, "Off with their heads." But Joseph makes this profound observation, "You intended to harm me, but God intended it for good to accomplish what is now being done, the saving of many lives" (Genesis 50:20).

If Joseph's brothers hadn't sold him into slavery, and had Potiphar's wife not put him in prison, his family, along with thousands of others, might have starved.

God knows what He's doing even when we don't. He keeps

us on the road to where we should be going even when it doesn't seem so to us. Sometimes we may feel that we have wandered off the path only to look up and realize that we are headed where God intended all along.

In a sense it's harder to get out of God's "ultimate" will than you might have thought. In fact, from the eternal point of view, it's impossible. The psalmist says, "All the days ordained for me were written in your book before one of them came to be" (Psalm 139:16). Your life story always proceeds as planned because God is the author who wrote the book.

JUST DO IT

CAN YOU think of three bad situations that later turned out to bring good? Spend some time praising and thanking God for His love and wisdom.

33
LOOKING FOR THE LOWLY

Brothers, think of what you were when you were called. Not many of you were wise by human standards; not many were influential; not many were of noble birth. But God chose the foolish things of this world to shame the wise; God chose the weak things of this world to shame the strong.

1 CORINTHIANS 1:26–27

GOD SEEMS TO RARELY VISIT THE rich and powerful. Oh, it does happen occasionally. One queen of England was fond of saying that she would make it into God's kingdom between the *M* and the *A* of the not "many." Remember, Paul didn't say not *any* noble; he said "not many." Still, in most cases it appears as if God looks down from heaven and says, "What lowly, unknown character can I raise up to glorify My name today?"

As a young Christian, I thought that our group's evangelism efforts should focus on celebrities. My theory was that the poster people could influence more folks for Christ than us ordinary-Joe types. Occasionally I would hear of a celebrity conversion, but I was usually disappointed that not many seemed to follow. That taught me an important lesson: God doesn't build His kingdom on the fragile backs of star power. Glitz doesn't go very far with the Lord, and Isaiah tells us why, "This is the one I esteem: he who is humble and contrite in spirit, and trembles at my word" (Isaiah 66:2).

It's human nature to admire the beauty of a shapely figure, the power and pleasure that comes from a fat bank account, and the glamour of royalty and stardom. When Congress holds hearings on the environment, who do they call to testify before the leaders of the free world? Forestry Ph.D.'s like Jane Fonda and Meryl Streep. Star power may rule on earth, but not in heaven. God is not impressed. It is a humble view of self and a respectful view of His word that gets His attention.

Luke 3 begins like the guestlist for this season's *Lifestyles of the Rich and Famous*. The seven most powerful men in the world are listed in order of descending prominence. Five men are Roman rulers, and two come from the world of religion.

First, there is the Caesar named Tiberius. He was the second emperor of the Roman Empire. And like all the Caesars, he demanded to be worshiped like a god. Then Pontius Pilate, the man who sent Jesus to His death while ruler over Judea and Samaria. Herod the ruler of Galilee is next. He was the Roman governor who had had John the Baptist beheaded for criticizing his marriage to his brother's wife. Then Philip, another Roman who ruled Iturea and Traconitus. He is remembered for his incredible building, including the magnificent city of Caesarea Phillipi. The last of the Roman rulers listed is Lysanias. He was tetrarch of a region called Abilene.

Next come our two religious leaders, Annas and Caiaphas. Annas was appointed to the position of high priest by a Roman governor and was the first to interrogate Jesus before His crucifixion. Caiaphas, who was Annas's son-in-law, saw Jesus next. He was the man who advised the Jews that it would be good if one man died for the people. Both men were involved in the arrest of Peter in Acts 4.

These seven men are a first-century who's who, and yet Luke tells us, "The word of God came to John, son of Zechariah, in the desert." God bypassed the famous and looked to the fameless. He preferred humility over royalty, deserting the palace and visiting the desert. The Word of God came to a locust-eating, animal-skin-wearing unknown named John.

Few people could name the five rulers and two religious leaders who were so prominent in the beginning of the first century, but millions remember John the Baptist. His legacy will live throughout eternity because God is not impressed by men of means, but He does highly regard "he who is humble and contrite in spirit, and trembles at my word." A humble heart is the only fertile ground for God's Word, and when it is planted there—and watered with tears of repentance—you can always count on a bumper crop.

JUST DO IT

CLOSE YOUR EYES and visualize yourself at the foot of the cross, looking up into the eyes of Jesus. Write down the observations God gives you as you compare yourself to His humble greatness.

34
DANIEL

You may have had to suffer grief in all kinds of trials. These have come so that your faith—of greater worth than gold, which perishes even though refined by fire—may be proved genuine and may result in praise, glory and honor when Jesus Christ is revealed.
1 PETER 1:6–7

WE LIVE IN AN AGE WHERE ALCOHOLISM is not a sin, it's a disease. Homosexuality is just a different sexual orientation. Many school children receive no test scores so as not to hurt their self-esteem. The Ten Commandments are reduced to "ten suggestions," and criminals are victims because they grew up under difficult circumstances.

According to Peter, difficult times are intended to make us better people, not worse. The heat of hard times is intended to refine us like gold, not forge us into monuments of godlessness.

The ancient goldsmith refined his metals by placing them in a heated vat. The white-hot fire underneath caused the impurities in the metal to rise to the top. The goldsmith would take a long thin ladle and skillfully scoop off the top layer of froth, separating it from the gold. He continued this process until he was able to look down in the pot and see his reflection. Then he knew the gold was pure.

Jesus may allow the heat of hard times to come our way, but they are only permitted to burn until we are made pure. As a wise master craftsman, He is able to use those flames to create His reflection in us, while knowing how much heat we can withstand before being consumed.

If there was ever a man who could have melted in the flames of hard times, it was Daniel. He was abducted from his family in his early teenage years by one of the most violent dictators who ever lived. He was taken hundreds of miles away from his home in Israel and raised in a world-renowned society of wickedness. The king forced him into a three-year retraining program designed specifically to change his way of thinking. His captors used a very sophisticated form of brainwashing. They changed his diet, his language, and even gave him a pagan name. At home he had been called Daniel, meaning "God is my judge," but in the apostate city of Babylon he was referred to as Belteshazzar, meaning "may Bel protect you."

They changed his geography, diet, language, and name, but they never changed Daniel's character. Daniel remained faithful to the God of his childhood. In his career he rose twice from obscurity to a position of near unlimited political power. In fact, Daniel grew up to be such an amazing man that the archangel Michael told him that he was "greatly beloved" in heaven.

He may have been greatly loved up in the wild blue yonder, but he was hated here on earth. His friends admired him, but his enemies, jealous of his accomplishments, loathed him. On one occasion the Scripture says that "the administrators and the satraps tried to find grounds for charges against Daniel in his conduct of government affairs, but they were unable to. They could find no corruption in him, because he was trustworthy and neither corrupt nor negligent." In frustration they had to conspire to make it against the law to pray in order to make Daniel a lawbreaker.

What a tremendous testimony it is when the enemies of God say, "We will never find any basis for charges against this man Daniel unless it has something to do with the law of his God" (Daniel 6:5). What an achievement it is when the only ammunition your enemies have is your own commitment to do what is right. The bait in the trap says a great deal about what the hunter expects to catch.

Daniel had plenty of excuses to throw in the moral towel as a teenager. He could have said, "I can't be held responsible, I'm a victim of my horrible environment." He could have given up as a grown man complaining, "God, I've been living for you and now I'm repaid by being punished for doing right," but Daniel didn't. He became the second-most-powerful man in the world, yet he never compromised in success or complained in failure. The hard times that for others might have been an excuse to give up, served only to make Daniel's testimony shine brighter both in his day and ours. Like a diamond in the jeweler's case, the flawless character of Daniel is best seen against the black background of Babylon.

As we race toward the return of Christ, it is likely our world will grow as dark as Daniel's. Some Christians will chose to curse the darkness; some will join it. Daniel chose to displace it by letting the light of Christ shine. Opportunities to shine like Daniel await all of us, and the good news is that the darker our world gets, the easier it will be for those around us to see our light.

JUST DO IT

MAKE A MENTAL list of the bait that Satan might use to lure you from Christ. Pray about each area of weakness. Take the steps necessary to fortify your character in these areas. Only you know your weak areas, so write your own and just do it; disconnect the cable, avoid a certain friend, deal with a habit, etc.

35
LIAR, LUNATIC, OR LORD

"What about you . . . who do you say that I am."
MATTHEW 16:15

TWO BRIGHT AND CHEERY YOUNG LADIES came calling on a Sunday a while back. As I opened my front door they smiled and said, "Hi, we're from the Church of Jesus Christ of Latter Day Saints and we'd like to talk to you about Jesus."

It caught them off guard when I responded, "You can tell me about Jesus, but you're not going to like it." Looking puzzled one young lady asked, "Why?" I told her that I was a Christian, and as if the conversation had gotten back on track, she raised her head and said, "So are we."

I knew neither were true.

There are ways to go about religious discussions that are like trying to unravel a rubber ball. You follow the knots and tangles that only lead you down to new tangled paths . . . or you can cut right to the quick. That's more my style.

The one question that gets to the point fastest is the one Jesus asked Peter: "Who do you say that I am?" Only Christians answer by saying, "You are God." Some say Jesus is "a" god, but only Christians proclaim him to be "the" God.

I told the young ladies that I wanted to start our discussion by talking about who Jesus was. Thinking that she had won a small victory, one of the girls said, "OK, you go first." Her victory evaporated when, just for fun, I said, "Jesus is the eschatological manifestation of the ground of our being, the kerygma in which we find the ultimate meaning of our interpersonal relationships or, in other words, God."

I was surprised to read this in a Charlotte paper, "New Testament scholars meet to pick a father for Jesus Christ." The three choices scheduled for debate were: (1) the Holy Spirit, (2) Joseph, and (3) an anonymous man.

The group was founded by Dr. Robert Funk and meets annually to discuss the claims of Christ and is made up of representatives from Notre Dame, Harvard, Eden Theological Seminary, and dozens of other schools. Funk predicted, "Few will find evidence to support a vote for the Holy Spirit." And who could doubt it when you learned the featured speaker's theme was "The Illegitimacy of Jesus."

Justifying the group's purpose, Funk said, "We are not interested in tearing down a Christian's faith, but in helping them realize where myths are myths. Some people are threatened . . . unless they feel there is solid historical evidence for everything they believe, they will not be able to believe it at all. That's a disease of the scientific age. It is only when mythology is understood to be factual that it becomes demonic."

From cute, young, all-American Mormons to apostate pedagogues, there is a wide range of opinion out there on the question of "Who is Jesus?" Christians stake their eternal lives on the fact that He is God, and they have tons of solid ground on which to stand.

The Bible clearly claims that Jesus is God. Here are just a few scriptures:

- "But about the Son he says, 'Your throne, O God, will last forever.'" (Hebrews 1:8)

- "For to us a child is born, to us a son is given . . . and he will be called Wonderful Counselor, Mighty God, Everlasting Father, Prince of Peace." (Isaiah 9:6)

- "We wait for the blessed hope—the glorious appearing of our great God and Savior, Jesus Christ." (Titus 2:13)

- "For by him all things were created: things in heaven and on earth, visible and invisible, whether thrones or powers or rulers or authorities; all things were created by him and for him." (Colossians 1:16)

- "I and the Father are one." (John 10:30)

- "If you really knew me, you would know my Father as well. From now on, you do know him and have seen him." (John 14:7)

- "In the beginning was the Word, and the Word was God. . . . The Word became flesh and made his dwelling among us." (John 1:1, 14)

Since the Bible leaves no wiggle room, we are forced to yield to C. S. Lewis's logic. Jesus obviously taught that he was God. That leaves us with only three possible options. Either Jesus was a brilliant liar, a deranged lunatic, or He is Lord of the universe.

Option 1 makes Jesus, not only a liar, but also a fool. He obtained no financial gain for His charade, in fact, He died a brutal death for a claim He could have easily retracted.

Option 2 makes Jesus a psychopath with delusions of grandeur. But could the brilliant teachings of Christ come from a nut case? Furthermore, could He have managed to conceal His insanity from His mother, brothers, and those who lived with Him for three and a half years? We are forced to conclude with Lewis that "you can shut him up for a fool, you can spit at him and kill him as a demon, or you can do as only Christians do, fall at His feet and call Him Lord and God."

After all was said and done, my Mormon friends found a fourth way to deal with the "who is Jesus" question. Instead of declaring Him liar, lunatic, or Lord, they just changed the subject as often as possible so they didn't have to think about it.

JUST DO IT

ON YOUR knees worship Jesus as your Lord and God. Write three of the above Scriptures on a note card and memorize them this week.

36
DYING TO LIVE

I have been crucified with Christ and I no longer live, but Christ lives in me. The life I live in the body, I live by faith in the Son of God, who loved me and gave himself for me.

GALATIANS 2:20

THE TRUE MEANING OF THE CROSS HAS been muddled in modern society. You see crosses on churches and on biker jackets. Almost everyone has at least one piece of jewelry in the shape of a cross.

What most people don't seem to get is that the cross is an instrument of death. It is an executioner's tool. It would make as much sense to wear a tiny silver electric chair or guillotine. In the age of death by lethal injection perhaps a golden hypodermic needle would say it better. The point is, the cross should remind us of death.

This association was not lost on the disciples. Jesus' words, no doubt, sent a cold chill through them as they heard Him say, "If anyone would come after me, he must deny himself and take up his cross daily and follow me" (Luke 9:23). The disciples had seen convicted criminals carry the instruments of their own deaths up the hill called Golgotha. They had heard the distant screams of anguish as the Roman soldiers pounded in those nine-inch spikes; first into the left hand, then the right, and finally the feet. They soon would witness the unforgettable sight of their own beloved Savior being marched up that hill to His death.

When Jesus explained to His followers that the price for following Him was a cross, I'm sure a feather would have been sufficient to knock the disciples over. If He had preached this sermon today, He might have said, "If anyone wants to come after me he must take up his electric chair." Then perhaps we would have heard someone in the church whisper in His ear, "Preacher, you'll catch more flies with sugar than you will with vinegar."

Jesus didn't offer much sugar. He didn't seem to worry about building self-esteem, and He certainly never promised prosperity. Indeed, He promised quite the opposite saying, "Foxes have holes and birds of the air have nests, but the Son of Man has no place to lay his head" (Luke 9:58). The point being, *I have nothing, do you expect to be treated better than the master?*

Today, in what has been described as the "new age," there are millions of books and tapes being sold each year that promise to help you find your "true self" and communicate with your "inner voice." The cross of Christ is intended to crucify "self" and silence that "inner voice." The true Christian life begins with death, as we lay our hopes, dreams, and desires at the foot of the cross. These were but the selfish dreams of a man or women who is now dead to self but alive to God. The old self could not be rehabilitated; it had to be crucified.

Our new nature is that of Christ's. Therefore we desire what He desires, we build what He is building, we love what He loves and hate what He hates. His life in us energizes us to go forward with no remorse for the death of our former "true self" or concern for future safety. We trust that Christ knows what he's doing with the new vessel He indwells and will do what is best as He does what He wishes.

When James Calvert went out to evangelize the cannibals on the island of Fiji, the captain shouted from the ship, "If you go out among the savages, you will lose your life and those with you." Calvert shouted back, "We died before we came here."

Herein is freedom from fear and the beginning of real life: when we learn that life in Christ begins by dying.

JUST DO IT

PRAYERFULLY THINK about what Christ may dream of doing through you. Consider which of your plans may be inconsistent with His will and pray that He will give you the ability to release them from your grasp.

37
PART OF THE MYSTERY

*For he chose us in him before the creation of the
world to be holy and blameless in his sight. In love he
predestined us to be adopted as his sons through Jesus
Christ, in accordance with his pleasure and will.*

EPHESIANS 1:4–5

*it's just like the shapes on my grandmother's rug
you can't see the pattern when you're too close up
from my point of view we are all far too human to see
it's part of the mystery*

LIFE HOLDS A LOT OF GREAT MYSTERIES. Plain and simple there are
some things we weren't meant to understand. Like why do we
park in a driveway and drive on a parkway? Or if I'm driving some
night at the speed of light and turn on my headlights, am I going
to be able to see anything? Where do my socks go when they dis-
appear in the dryer? Why did kamikazes wear helmets? Think
about it.

I heard a man tell a new convert that the Bible has the
answer to everything. Sorry, that's not exactly true. Yes, it does tell
us everything we need to know to live godly lives. But in several
instances the Bible creates new problems. Take for instance the
whole predestination issue. What do you do with a verse like this
one: "Yet, before the twins were born or had done anything good
or bad—in order that God's purpose in election might stand: not
by works but by the one who calls—she was told, . . . 'Jacob I
loved, but Esau I hated'" (Romans 9:11–13).

There seems to be a fairness issue that crops up here. The fun part of election is that God loved us before we were even born. He's planned all the tiny details of our lives including that we would follow Jesus. Then, just when you're really enjoying this concept, it occurs to you this is a two-edged sword. If predestination guarantees the salvation of some, doesn't it seal the damnation of others?

When you read a verse like this you're hoping to eventually get to an explanation that reads, "God looked down the tunnel of time and saw that Esau wouldn't believe but Jacob would." Unfortunately, the explanation the apostle Paul gives only throws gasoline on the fairness fire. "God has mercy on whom he wants to have mercy, and he hardens whom he wants to harden" (Romans 9:18). Just when you're about to raise your hand in God's classroom to register your complaint, Paul slaps your intellectual face with, "Who are you, O man, to talk back to God?" *I guess he told us.*

I've heard some people explain election by saying, "It's like a door that when your facing it, it says, "Whosoever will," but when you pass through it and look back it says, "You were chosen." Others have explained predestination with the previously mentioned tunnel-of-time theory. But you can't get God off the fairness hook with this, because God created the tunnel and seems to be in charge of everything that passes through it. If He knew who would reject Him, He didn't have to create them. That brings us to conclude it may not be our job to get God off the fairness hook. Maybe it's just too big a job for our small minds to handle.

There was once a wandering man who made his way to the king's door in the middle of winter. Freezing in the cold, he begged for the king to let him in. The king said, "You may come in but first tell me why you are blowing on your hands." The wanderer replied, "I blow on them to warm them, your Majesty."

"Come in," said the king, "and dine with me."

All was going well at dinner until the soup came. The wandering man lifted the bowl to his face and began to blow on it. The king asked, "Sir, is your soup not hot enough to suit you?" The man replied, "Your Majesty, the soup is too hot, I'm blowing on it to cool it." At this the king launched from his seat and commanded, "Take this liar to the dungeon, for he claims that he can blow hot to cold and cold to hot." Of course, the man never really claimed to blow different temperatures. He only offered that his breath could warm cold hands and cool hot soup. Both are true, even if the king's limited knowledge of science would not permit him to understand it.

When it comes to election, it is quite possible that we simply fall into the same unfortunate category as the ignorant king. When the Bible indicates that God chooses some, while at the same time He is fair, both are true even if we aren't able to understand it. After all, Jesus told His disciples there were some things they were "not yet ready to bear." Maybe the answers that come from the issue of election are things we really wouldn't want to be told, like when and how we will die. Or maybe that our universe is in reality only the size of an atom that is part of the molecular structure of another giant universe. If that were true, would you really want to know it?

As can be predicted, some people aren't willing to leave it at that. I can still hear that girl say, "If that's the way God is, I'm not going to believe in Him." To me it seems rather silly to stamp your feet and throw a fit just because God is doing something you don't understand, and He hasn't given you a satisfactory explanation yet. For me, I'm willing to let it rest with, "God is fair and He knows what He's doing." Jesus will probably clue us in when we get to heaven. I'm banking on being a lot smarter then.

JUST DO IT

HERE ARE some great verses on the sovereignty of God. Mark them in your Bible because it's essential to know who is in charge, even if we can't understand how He does it: Romans 9:14–24, Psalms 135:6, and Jeremiah 18:6.

38
TO TELL YOU THE TRUTH

For prophecy never had its origin in the will of man, but men spoke from God as they were carried along by the Holy Spirit.

2 PETER 1:21

I'M A LITTLE SKEPTICAL BY NATURE. I believe God can still do miracles today. But I would dare say that a lot of what we see that passes for miracles today is really smoke and mirrors.

When you see people getting healed on television, normally what happens is a crippled person is helped up to the podium in a wheelchair. He or she gets a slap on the head, then rises up and walks. That's great, but I'd be more impressed if once in a while you'd see someone with no legs get up and walk. After all, on a couple of occasions Jesus even healed people who were dead. Now that's healing!

Today it's tough to tell if you are seeing the genuine article or not. The fortune tellers and psychics present you with the same kind of dilemma. The advice and predictions they make are virtually unverifiable. For instance, these are a few horoscopes I saw this morning in the paper: "Enjoyable times are ahead, but you awaken aware of the importance of financial solvency." This one's true for me every morning: "Get in touch with your inner voice, perhaps through dreams or simply stopping to smell the roses."

When I read stuff like this I don't smell roses, I smell something fishy. How do you ever verify if this person is telling the truth. My "inner voice" tells me that if you want to know the truth and get some good solid advice, look to God's Word.

The Old Testament prescribes an ingeniously simple test for determining what is truth from God or the imagination of man. The Lord says, "If what a prophet proclaims in the name of the LORD does not take place or come true, that is a message the LORD has not spoken" (Deuteronomy 18:20–22).

This test is based on a simple principle: Only God knows the future because He sovereignly planned it. Some people think that Satan knows the future, too, but the only future events he knows of are the ones he has read about in the Bible. Satan doesn't possess God's omni-attributes and neither do his minions. The only way the powers of darkness predict the future is the same way I might predict that I'm going to eat a Big Mac. First, I make the prediction, then I get in the car and drive to McDonald's. Thus, "I'm a prophet." If God's simple test for truth were in operation today, we would have fewer prophets. Then again, maybe not. As vague as their watered-down predictions are, it is impossible to tell if they ever come true.

But that's not true with God! The predictions in His Word are not that way. Scripture is filled with detailed prophecies that verify the truth of the Bible. For instance, His Word gives us scientific facts hundreds of years before discovery. At a time when everyone in the world believed the planet was flat, Isaiah told us the world was a "circle" (40:22). Two thousand years after Isaiah's prediction, Columbus, upon reading this passage, persuaded Spain's Queen Isabella to allow him to search for a shorter route to India. At a time when many believed that the Earth was held up by a giant who stood on the back of a turtle, Job told us that "he suspends the earth over nothing" (Job 26:7).

His word is also reliable in its prediction of historical events. Consider, for example, this account of the crucifixion spoken eight hundred years before this form of torture ever entered the heart of a Roman soldier: "My God, my God, why have you forsaken me? . . . I am poured out like water, and all my bones are out of joint. My heart has turned to wax; it has melted away within me. . . . They have pierced my hands and my feet. I can count all my bones; people stare and gloat over me. They divide my garments among them and cast lots for my clothing" (Psalm 22:1, 14, 16).

In all, there are more than ten details of Christ's crucifixion foretold here. And just as amazing, you could have known the date of this event by reading Daniel 9:25–26.

There are hundreds of examples of the Bible's prophetical and historical accuracy. Each points us to the divine source of its authorship.

Theologians sometimes refer to the above as the internal proofs of the inspiration of Scripture. They are incredible, but no more incredible than those often overlooked external proofs of the Bible's authorship. For instance, Luke tells us that John's father, Zachariah, was chosen by lot to perform temple duty. While serving as priest, Zachariah encountered an angel that promised him a son and made it impossible for Zachariah to speak (Luke 1:8–23). Now these events were written of and widely circulated in Zachariah's hometown at a time when eyewitnesses were alive and temple records were still around to deny these events if they were not true. Certainly the Jewish leaders would have blown the whistle if they could.

Likewise, Jesus came out of a guarded tomb and appeared to more than five hundred people. Many of these eyewitnesses became martyrs for their faith. You can be certain that if the Romans and Jews could have produced the body of Christ, they surely would have drug it through the streets of Jerusalem.

The enemies of God have long looked for opportunities to prove the Word of God in error. No other book has been so attacked or so revered in history. Yet this book continues to confound those who hate it and bless those who love it. Believers know that if the Bible is trustworthy in matters of prophecy, science, and history, it is also trustworthy as a guide for our daily decisions.

JUST DO IT

LOOK UP these amazing prophecies and their fulfillments.

Genesis 3:15 and Galatians 4:4
Micah 5:2 and Matthew 2:1
Isaiah 7:14 and Matthew 1:18
Jeremiah 31:15 and Matthew 2:16
Isaiah 53:4 and Matthew 8:16–17

39
THE GOOD SHEPHERD

"I am the good shepherd; I know my sheep and my sheep know me—just as the Father knows me and I know the Father—and I lay down my life for the sheep."

JOHN 10:14–15

THERE MAY BE NO BETTER WAY TO experience the love that Jesus has for His children than by reading and meditating on what is found in John 10. Jesus describes Himself in terms that first-century saints must have related to immediately. He calls Himself the Good Shepherd.

Shepherding was a common profession in those days and one that brought to mind immediate mental images. Jesus referred to Himself in many other ways, from the "Alpha and Omega" to the "Water of Life," but no other depiction of Christ is as loving and tender as that given in the story of the Good Shepherd.

Contrast (comparing differences between one thing and another) is a teaching tool Jesus often used to make His points. In Matthew 13 He contrasts the different types of soil. In Luke 6 He talks about the wise and foolish servant. The sheep and the goats are juxtaposed in Matthew 25. And in this sermon, He contrasts the good shepherd with the thief.

The thief is the slug who enters the sheep pen by climbing the wall. He, like so many of the false religions of the world, attempts to enter the sheepfold by his own self-made illegitimate ways. His mission, in Christ's words, is "to steal and kill." He has no real desire to protect or serve the sheep. *He wants to eat them.*

There is a classic episode of *The Twilight Zone* that I love. Aliens come to Earth under the guise of making friends. They offer the heads of state a large book written in alienese. It takes a while, but the translators eventually figure out that the cover says *To Serve Man*. To the delight of the unsuspecting Earthlings, they offer to take whoever wishes on a vacation trip to their planet. No one is surprised, after all, these alien guys just want to "serve" man. Furthermore, everyone who goes, loves the alien planet so much that they don't want to come back. If you haven't seen it or guessed by now, the alien *To Serve Man* book is a cookbook. Likewise, when the thief says he "loves the sheep," what he's saying is that he likes lamb chops.

In sharp distinction, the good shepherd doesn't kill the sheep; he lays down his life for them. When the wolves and lions come he doesn't think about himself. He thinks only of his sheep. His life is focused on making sure his lambs live life to its fullest. In the face of danger the thief preserves himself, but self-preservation is the last thing on the good shepherd's mind.

For the good shepherd, fighting wolves and lions is only a small part of the job. Most days are filled with searching for water and green grass or leading the way into the city for supplies. For the most part, the shepherd's job is to sit back and let sheep be sheep. Plain old sheep nature and common sense does most of the work. It's not necessary for the shepherd to say, "Chew that piece of grass there," or "You're thirsty now, have a drink of water." The shepherd only reaches out with his staff or raises his voice when a distracted lamb is getting ready to walk over a cliff or is wandering too far from the flock. Literal sheep do what comes naturally, and so do God's figurative sheep —the believers.

The Good Shepherd allows us to follow our new nature. And that nature instinctively leads us into the safe haven of God's will. If all is going well, there is no need for the shepherd to raise his voice. Times of silence indicate that all is going according to the shepherd's plan. He only raises his voice or staff in times of danger, or if it is necessary to seek food in another direction.

Some people think they need to hear the shepherd's voice

in every tiny decision—and if they don't, they fear that he has abandoned them. *This is a mistake!*

We shouldn't expect God to tell us to wear the green shirt or the blue one. As long as we dress in a way that keeps us safe from moral harm, we don't need a word from the shepherd, nor should we expect one. If we are keeping our ears open in prayer but hear nothing, we can continue in the confidence that our Spirit-led, new nature is sufficient for almost every important decision we make. If we wander too near to danger, we have the assurance that the shepherd who loves us enough to lay down His own life, will speak up in such a way that is impossible for His lambs to miss.

JUST DO IT

MAKE A MENTAL list of a few of the things you trust the Good Shepherd to watch over for you. Spend a moment acknowledging your dependency on Jesus. Thank Him for His amazing love.

40

No More Problems

Consider it pure joy, my brothers, whenever you face trials of many kinds, because you know that the testing of your faith develops perseverance. Perseverance must finish its work so that you may be mature and complete, not lacking anything.

JAMES 1:2–4

I MADE A DECISION TO FOLLOW CHRIST at the age of seventeen in a closet at Hillcrest High School. Eddie DeGarmo, my friend and music partner, had made a commitment the previous Sunday at a David Wilkerson crusade. He was determined it was my turn next. Not wanting to let my friends hear me talking about Jesus or talking to someone who was, we ducked into a vacant closet. Eddie told me two things. First, "Dana, if you decide to follow Christ, He will forgive your sins," and second, "You will never have any more problems." It sounded great to me, so I moved some brooms around and told Jesus that from this day forward I intended to serve Him.

I was feeling great for the rest of the school day but afterward, things went south. You see, Eddie and I were already playing in a band at the time that had a recording contract with London Records (the recording company of the Rolling Stones and ZZ Top). Our music wasn't Christian. In fact, it was downright pagan. This was an observation that until our evening rehearsal had alluded my notice.

I was singing a song I had written, when it suddenly occurred to me that the words were pornographic. I put down my guitar and went to speak to my manager about my moral dilemma. It didn't go over well. With an angry, red face he said, "Dana, you've got a big decision to make, pal. Do you still want to be a rock star or have you made up your mind to become a religious fanatic?"

I hated the way that sounded. It had only been four short hours since I had ducked into a closet so that no one could hear me even discussing Jesus. Now my manager was challenging me to pick between being a Christian or being Elvis. (Hey, I'm from Memphis.) I was starting to suspect Ed was mistaken about that "no problems" promise.

A few short months later I was kicked out of the band, losing the recording contract and all the "benefits" that went with it. Our band wasn't ready to be sanitized, and in one of those rare moments of poetic justice, Eddie was forced out, too.

Undaunted by losing our recording contract, we found Christian musicians to take the place of the missing musicians. It took a while but soon we were rocking as hard as ever. In fact, better, now that we were singing about Christ. We attempted to resume our appearances on the nightclub circuit but soon found out that Jesus rock and the nightlife didn't mix. It seems our music had a negative effect on beer and alcohol sales. It didn't take long before I was sure Ed didn't know what he was talking about when he promised "no more problems."

"Have no fear," I told Brother Eddie, "we need to fellowship with our brethren and sistern." After six months of church attendance I was starting to speak and understand some Christianese, though not fluently. I said, "Brother Eddie, upon yonder corner standeth a large church in which we can minister to the saints." Before I knew what happened, I was explaining my new vision to the pastor and one of his assistants. I told them, "Brothers, we've got a 'little gospel group' [Hey, don't get the idea I was lying. It simply fell under the heading of being as wise as a serpent when you have enough wisdom to avoid descriptions like 'Jesus rock band.'] and we would like to come over Sunday night and *share*."

That Sunday night we did share, briefly. We played eight bars of one song at 105 decibels. Quickly, men starting making their way toward the stage from the back of the room. I was a young Christian, but I had enough discernment to see they were not sharing our joy. I leaned over to Eddie and asked, "What do you think these guys want?" He answered, "I think they want to lay hands on us." He was correct. In just a short moment we were picking up our gear in the parking lot and packing the truck. I was again thinking, *Ed, you must have been lying to me in that closet.*

It wasn't really his fault. You see when Eddie made that promise, he had only been a Christian for twenty-four hours and apparently he had had a pretty good day. Those who follow Christ for the long haul soon learn that following Him adds new problems to your life that you never imagined. Problems not only *might* happen, they *will*. The promise of problems is a promise that is certain and should be considered our privilege. "For it has been granted to you on behalf of Christ not only to believe on him, but also to suffer for him" (Philippians 1:29). But never forget that even if He didn't die to take us away from problems, He did die to give us power to overcome them. "In all these things we are more than conquerors through him who loved us. For I am convinced that neither death nor life, neither angels nor demons, neither the present nor the future, nor any powers, neither height nor depth, nor anything else in all creation, will be able to separate us from the love of God that is in Christ Jesus our Lord" (Romans 8:37–39).

Christians are called to graduate to heaven from the school of hard knocks. The blows we take only serve to smooth off the rough edges, pounding us into Christ's image. Losing my recording contract and band, along with being booted out of a church, turned out to be my first semester in that school. And I still haven't graduated!

JUST DO IT

MAKE A LIST of some of the hard knocks Jesus took in coming down out of heaven to suffer for you. Now make a list of some of the more recent knocks you've experienced. Prayerfully consider what God may have been trying to teach you through each of them.

41

You Can't Take It with You

> *"Do not store up for yourselves treasures on earth, where moth and rust destroy, and where thieves break in and steal. But store up for yourselves treasures in heaven, where moth and rust do not destroy, and where thieves do not break in and steal."*
>
> MATTHEW 6:19–20

THE CAMPUS LIFE DIRECTOR REENACTED the life of Job for his club in this way. He asked club members to take five plain index cards and list their most cherished possession, talent, or relationship at the top of each. When the small commotion ended he said, "Now imagine this, you picked up your girlfriend and joined your friends at a party. That night there was an earthquake and the roof caved in, killing everyone at the party but you. You were paralyzed head to toe but survived. Now, if you're holding a card bearing the name of a friend, drop it to the floor. If you're holding a card that has a talent listed or career hope that you couldn't achieve as a paraplegic, drop that card." The kids moaned and most of the cards fell to their feet.

Then the discussion leader said, "Your whole family visited the dentist and he intentionally gave them AIDS. If you are holding a family member's card, let that card fall." The nightmare of tragedies continued until only one teen held one card. Of course, at the top of that card was written the name of Jesus Christ. There is absolutely nothing else in life that cannot be destroyed or stolen.

Jim Elliot understood this when he said, "He is no fool that gives what he cannot keep to gain what he cannot lose." Jim later lost his life serving on the mission field, but Jesus could never be taken from him.

Shortly after my conversion to Christ, I had a strange dream. Normally I don't put much stock in my dreams, but this one seemed different. I heard someone yelling to me who appeared to be standing on the ceiling. He was saying, "Be careful, you are going to fall." I argued at length that it was he who was in danger of falling, not me. My case fell apart when he pointed at an upside-down chandelier standing next to me.

At this revelation, I became fearful and tried desperately to crawl on hands and knees across the ceiling and down the wall. Each time I made progress going down, I either slipped or lost my grasp of the wall and drifted slowly back up to the ceiling. Eventually my friends on the floor reached up and reeled me in like a small Goodyear blimp. They sat me in a chair, but its weight was not enough to keep me on the ground. They filled my pockets with coins, but still more weight was required. They stacked books on my lap, along with a stereo and guitar. Finally, I was anchored.

It was then I woke up and rolled from my bed to the floor to pray. Very clearly, I felt like Jesus was saying, "Dana, if you want to look and live like the rest of the unbelieving world, you can do it by weighting yourself down with possessions. But if you wish to fly above the world, simply let go of things and your true nature will carry you toward heaven."

A young, new pastor in Arkansas was unable to afford a suit. A sympathetic funeral director offered to let him come over to the mortuary and pick one from the hundreds he kept for use on the deceased. The pastor picked out a handsome blue one. Admiring it in the dressing room mirror, he went to place his hands in the pockets. It was then that a sober fact hit. These suits were not made with pockets because the customers who usually wore them had no need. Jesus Christ is the only treasure that will accompany us past the grave. It is wise to invest heavily in this future.

JUST DO IT

MAKE A MENTAL list of the five most important things, people, or abilities in your life. Then prayerfully consider how temporary and fragile each of them is.

42
GUILT AND CONVICTION

One thing I do: Forgetting what is behind and straining toward what is ahead, I press on toward the goal to win the prize for which God has called me heavenward in Christ Jesus.

PHILIPPIANS 3:13–14

THERE IS A LOT OF CONFUSION AMONG Christians about guilt. People don't know when to feel guilty or why. Strictly speaking Christians should never wrestle with guilt, and later on I will tell you why.

As a young Christian I struggled with my affluent upbringing. No, we weren't rich, but we had nice clothes, plenty of food, and a car. When I read the Bible, it gave me the impression that the disciples were dirt poor and this seemed to add a degree of spirituality to their lives. I, on the other hand, was doomed to never experience this higher plain of poverty-elevated spirituality unless I renounced my possessions. That's what I did.

I decided to make friends who were poor in a really bad part of Memphis. I even joined a poverty-stricken church. It was the kind of place that had been robbed so often, the deacons were replaced by bouncers. Only the bravest in our fellowship were willing to close their eyes during prayer. If you saw holy hands reaching to heaven, it very well could be a robbery in progress.

I continued attending this church for several months until I concluded it wasn't making me feel less guilt about my blessed upbringing. It only made me feel more guilty because I dreaded Sunday mornings!

Technically speaking, guilt is remorse about past sins. But sins in our past shouldn't be our main concern. Scripture tells us why. First, "We have been made holy through the sacrifice of the body of Jesus Christ once for all" (Hebrews 10:10).

When I hear someone say, "I've done such terrible things in the past that Christ couldn't possibly forgive me," I know this is a person who doesn't place a lot of value in the death of Christ. What he's saying is, "Never mind that the eternal, sinless lamb of God was sacrificed in my place. It was not enough to cover my debt."

A quick rundown of the Hebrews Faith Hall of Fame in chapter 11 should put any such nonsense to rest. Abraham is in the hall of fame, but he was a liar. Likewise, Jacob deceived his own brother. Moses and David were murderers. Samson a whoremonger.

Is your sin greater than these? Not likely. Do you know what that means? There is still room for you in the Faith Hall of Fame.

The second reason we have no reason to punish ourselves with past sins is simple: they are in the past. The future is coming, and we can prepare for it. The present is here, and we must live in it, but the past is gone, and we cannot reach back and affect it.

Paul, who describes himself as the "chief of all sinners," understood this principle saying, "One thing I do: Forgetting what is behind and straining toward what is ahead, I press on toward the goal" (Philippians 3:13). We must all learn to forget the past in order to press on to the future.

So what part of our sin should we worry about? Not past sin, unless it is to learn from a mistake. We should focus on present and future sin, allowing guilt to live in the unreachable past where it belongs.

The Holy Spirit uses *conviction,* not guilt, to make us aware of our sin. I've found that most Christians are confused about guilt and conviction. They think they're twin brothers, but the fact is, they are not even related.

Guilt is a leach that sucks the vitality out of our lives by latching hold of the past. Conviction is a lifeguard that lives in the present. Guilt is a tool used by Satan; conviction is a tool of the Holy

Spirit. Guilt is intended to immobilize the Christian; conviction is intended to prod you to obedience. Guilt is a worldly sorrow that leads to death; conviction is a Godly sorrow that leads to life. Guilt is transfixed with self; conviction points you to Christ.

A former president of Youth for Christ used to say that most of the homeless people you see living out of cardboard boxes suffer less from a lack of good fortune and more from an abundance of guilt. They demonstrate their poverty in public trying to cleanse themselves of the past. As they lay in pools of excrement, they are screaming to the world, "Punish me, punish me, I'm a loser!"

You can punish yourself for the past or you can accept Christ's sacrifice for payment in full. You can become immobilized in your own self-pity or you can leap for joy in the wake of Christ's complete cleansing.

Will you acknowledge the eternal value of Christ's death or will you insult Him by living as if His death was not enough?

JUST DO IT

HERE ARE two great verses. Write them on a note card and carry them in your pocket or purse for a week.

In your love you kept me from the pit of destruction; you have put all my sins behind your back.
ISAIAH 38:17

As far as the east is from the west, so far has he removed our transgressions from us.
PSALM 103:12

43
Amazing Grace

But by the grace of God I am what I am, and his grace to me was not without effect. No, I worked harder than all of them—yet not I, but the grace of God that was with me.
1 CORINTHIANS 15:10

THE MOST INTENSELY PERSONAL song I've written is "Casual Christian." The chorus goes, "I don't wanna be, I don't wanna be a casual Christian, because I want to light up the night, with an everlasting light. I don't what to live a casual Christian life." This song is special to me because it comes from experience. I don't want to disappoint you, but there have been times when I have felt stranded in a spiritual wilderness. This chorus was written at just such a time. It was a cry for help.

All Christians go through wilderness experiences. John says, "If we claim to be without sin, we deceive ourselves and the truth is not in us" (1 John 1:8). No, we don't plan to fall or try to dismiss those dry times as normal. They are far from what God has planned for a normal Christian life. Thankfully, He has provided the grace we need to avoid them.

Grace has been defined in a variety of different ways. Consequently, there has been a lot of confusion about what part it plays in making us more like Christ (sanctification). Some have defined *grace* by its acronym, God's Riches At Christ's Expense. This is certainly an accurate definition, but it is somewhat inadequate at providing any clues to finding your way out of a desert.

A more useful definition of grace may be "God's enabling power to be holy." Grace is anything and everything that empowers us to do that which was impossible to do when we were "dead in our trespasses," namely to be holy. Paul tells us that through Christ "we have gained access by faith into this grace in which we now stand" (Romans 5:2). The point is, our faith is the key that unlocks the storeroom of grace, giving us access to the power that strengthens our otherwise weary spiritual legs.

Now the question arises, how can I get more grace when I need it, especially when I'm wandering in the wilderness of sin? The answer is that God has provided us with special turbocharged channels for getting lots of grace and fast. Theologians call them the "means of grace." These "means" are simply the avenues by which God funnels enabling power into our lives. Strictly speaking, God uses "all things," even our sin to make us holy (Romans 8:28–29), but His primary force in changing us is received by those wonderful little rivers called the "means of grace."

They are:

1. *The Word of God.* It is said that this book will keep you from sin or sin will keep you from this book. The psalmist says, "Your word is a lamp to my feet and a light for my path" (Psalm 119:105). Do you want to find the way out? Light up the way with God's Word.

2. *Prayer.* Sir Isaac Newton said that he could take his telescope and look millions and millions of miles into space. Then he added, "But when I lay it aside, go into my room, shut the door and get down on my knees in earnest prayer, I see more of heaven and feel closer to the Lord than if I were assisted by all the telescopes on Earth."

   It shouldn't be overlooked that in the greatest of all spiritual warfare passages, Ephesians 6, Paul tells us, "above all" we must remember to pray. Prayer is so often our last resort rather than our first resource, and what a pity, especially when you consider it gives us access to the infinite power of heaven.

3. *Fellowship.* There is only one institution in the world that has been promised divine protection from the

gates of hell, and that is the church (Matthew 16:18). Governments may crumble, families may disintegrate, but Christ has promised that the church will prevail.

One of the many reasons that the church is a safe haven from Satan is because of its structure. God has appointed shepherds who are given the divine charge of watching over His sheep (1 Peter 5:2). If you refuse the care of these shepherds you will be missing an essential source of enabling power. No Christian ever stands long for Jesus who is not connected to the fellowship of a local church.

4. *Service.* God has given each of us in the body of Christ gifts and abilities (1 Corinthians 12—14). These gifts are called grace gifts because they are God's little packages of grace and we are the mailmen. Don't worry about searching for these gifts. Look to love people and these gifts will find you. I love what Mother Teresa often says, "I am a little pencil in the writing hand of God, sending a love letter to the world." Make it your goal to send God's love to those around you. You will receive more grace than anyone you choose to bless.

When someone tells me he is struggling spiritually, I only have to ask, "When did you cut yourself off from one or more of these supercharged channels of grace?" It is true 100 percent of the time that his trip to the desert began the day he took himself off God's grace life-support system.

JUST DO IT

HAVE YOU developed a habit of daily Bible study? Are you listening for the Spirit's voice in prayer? Are you a functioning part of a church? Have you made it your goal to help others as you see their needs? If you are doing all of these things you will find it impossible to wander far from God's will.

44
THE SWORD OF THE SPIRIT

The word of God is living and active. Sharper than any double-edged sword.

HEBREWS 4:12

W.C. FIELDS WAS A CANTANKEROUS comedian, notorious for his smoking, drinking, and hatred of children. It was a surprise when a fellow train passenger spotted him reading the Bible. When asked about it, Fields responded, "I'm looking for loopholes."

It's hard to think of a worse reason to be in the Word than this, though I've tried. Through the years I've kept a list of the most bogus reasons for reading the Bible. Here is my top five:

1. A lady calling the psychic hot line says she's searching for her astrological sign.

2. A self-righteous preacher said reading the Bible helps you to point out your friend's faults.

3. A group of hippie holdouts from the 1960s say they read the Bible for the great wardrobe suggestions.

4. A lady's group from Chicago searches the Scripture for new recipes.

And finally the worst reason for reading the Bible is offered by an anonymous history professor:

5. For the sex and violence.

Of course, the best reason for reading God's Word comes from the Bible itself. In our dark, violence-prone world of spiritual warfare, the Bible is our only offensive weapon. Paul, in Ephesians 6, tells us that the battle we are fighting is a spiritual battle. "For our struggle is not against flesh and blood, but against the rulers, against the authorities, against the powers of this dark world and against the spiritual forces of evil in the heavenly realms" (Ephesians 6:12). Sometimes it's easy to think that our enemies are the pornographers, abortionists, or profane entertainers of this world. But they're not the problem, they're the symptom. They are simply pawns being used by hideously powerful, yet intelligent fallen angels. Organized against us by Satan, their goal is to destroy the kingdom of God and all who are seeking its benefits. But we've nothing to fear, God has given us all we need to fight and win the spiritual war.

We have the belt of truth, the breastplate of righteousness. We've got shoes that are ready to march, a shield of faith, a helmet of salvation, and finally, the only *weapon* mentioned, we have the sword of the Spirit.

God's sword is the only tool a saint needs to cut through the murky issues of the day. "For the word of God is living and active. Sharper than any double-edged sword, it penetrates even to the dividing soul and spirit, joints and marrow; judges the thoughts and attitudes of the heart" (Hebrews 4:12).

It cuts through the abortion issue telling us that it's God who knit us together in our mother's womb (Psalm 139:13). It was John the Baptist, not an unviable tissue mass, that was filled with the Spirit in his mother's womb (Luke 1:15). It is the sword of the Spirit that slices quickly through gay and lesbian issues telling us it is "detestable" for a man to lie with a man as one does with a woman (Leviticus 18:22). The Bible speaks on welfare issues saying, "If a man will not work, he shall not eat" (2 Thessalonians 3:10). To the pornographer it says that to look at a woman with lust is the same sin as adultery (Matthew 5:28).

We are not losing the spiritual battle in America because we don't have the weapon we need, it's because we've failed to pick it up and use it. Recently, I played a cruel joke on an adult Sunday

School class. As I began our study I asked the class to turn to the Book of Hezekiah and almost everyone made a futile search for a book in the Bible that doesn't exist. While more than 80 percent of Americans believe in God, very few study His Word regularly.

Learn God's Word. Arm yourself with truth. Don't go out to fight armed only with opinions or good intentions, for God's Word is an unstoppable offensive weapon against the real forces of evil.

JUST DO IT

MEMORIZE PSALM 1. What is the reward for delighting in God's Word? What happens to the ungodly?

45
Already There

"But seek first his kingdom and his righteousness, and all these things will be given to you as well. Therefore do not worry about tomorrow, for tomorrow will worry about itself. Each day has enough trouble of its own."

MATTHEW 6:33–34

PEOPLE FACE THE FUTURE IN DIFFERENT ways. Some people are fearful. *Saturday Night Live*'s A. Whitney Brown handles it through laughter. While speaking of the possibility of global destruction, he remarked, "When I put all this into the big picture, I have to say that the whole nuclear issue is blown way out of proportion. I have a feeling our descendants are going to look back at this entire arms race brouhaha and laugh their feelers off."

The Bible tells us not to face the future with laughter or fear. In fact, Jesus doesn't want us to deal with the future at all. He wants us to leave it to Him.

Jesus had a great deal to say to us about the future in His Sermon on the Mount. Most of what he said came in the form of warnings concerning worry. Worry sucks the vitality out of the Christian life unless it is exposed to the daylight of God's Word. There are three important truths that the disciple of Jesus must embrace in order to live and serve in perfect peace.

First, take one day at a time. In Matthew 6:34 the Lord warns that we mustn't worry about the future because "each day has enough trouble of its own." It has been said that all of us are able to bear the burden of today. It's when burdens of tomorrow are bundled with today's that our backs are broken. Most worries of the future are merely human speculations that never come to pass anyway.

Nature is set up on a twenty-four-hour cycle that allows us to deal with problems the way God intended. Perhaps the Eskimos could teach us something about this. If you ask an Eskimo how old he is, he is likely to tell you "one day." That's because Eskimos view sleep like death and awakening like birth. Each day they are born afresh to deal with the stressful hardships of the arctic life.

Jesus also taught us to "seek first his kingdom and his righteousness" (Matthew 6:33) instead of trying to seek answers concerning the future. In a sense it can be said that it is inappropriate to preoccupy ourselves with God's long-term will. We should be seeking first His kingdom.

Now, this is important, so read slowly. It is impossible to get out of God's will while you are diligently seeking Him. But if you wish to do His will, don't seek to know His will, seek *to know God*.

There used to be a Greyhound bus commercial that said, "Take the bus and leave the driving to us." In regard to the future it is important to take hold of Him, and He will take care of the driving.

The third thing to understand is that humans were designed to be linear. We have distinct human limitations. We are finite creatures with one point of beginning that started our clocks. As a result, we view time as running in a line. It's like driving through rolling hills. We cannot see past the next one until we drive to the top and look over. We cannot see our final destination, just the next bit of highway and the next hill to climb. Furthermore, Jesus asks, which of you "can add a single hour to his life" (Matthew 6:27), pointing out that even if we could see what was ahead we are powerless to change it.

God sits at the top of the mountain and sees the beginning of the journey, the points in-between, and the destination—all at the same time. Christ's power is unlimited. He is not bound by space or time. He is eternal.

He tells the Pharisees in John 8, that He is indeed the great "I am" who spoke to Moses in the burning bush (verse 58). Moses understood that the "I am" was a sovereign God who lived outside of the confines of time. He saw the future as if it were the past. His dwelling place was in the eternal present. This, of course, means that Jesus ruled in the past, He rules today, and He rules the future. Because of His mastery of time and great love for us, we need not fear the future. Our precious Jesus is already there, and He is waiting for us to join Him.

JUST DO IT

LIST FIVE of your greatest fears for the future. Then lay them before the feet of the great "I Am" in prayer. After you're through praying, crumple the paper, and put it in the trash.

46
Ready for Either

The third time he said to him, "Simon son of John, do you love me?" Peter was hurt because Jesus asked him the third time, "Do you love me?" He said, "Lord, you know all things; you know that I love you." Jesus said, "Feed my sheep."

JOHN 21:17

AN ANCIENT ROMAN COIN WAS FOUND bearing the picture of an ox. Two objects stood before the ox, a plow and an altar. The intended message was that the noble ox was ready to serve either by those long, tedious days and hours in the field or in that sudden and final moment of self-sacrifice at the altar.

The apostle Peter was a disciple who was ready for either. He boasted to Christ "emphatically" at the last supper that, "Even if I have to die with you, I will never disown you" (Mark 14:31). There is no doubt that when these words came out of Peter's mouth, he meant them. Proving as much, later that same evening in the Garden of Gethsemane, Peter pulled his sword and took on the temple guards. He alone tried to prevent Jesus' arrest. Yet, sometime before dawn, his enthusiasm for dying evaporated. He denied even knowing Jesus three times.

Peter learned what most disciples of Christ must; that it's sometimes easier to die for Christ than to live for Him. It is easy, in a Spirit-inspired moment to make bold pronouncements of devotion and sacrifice, but it is far more difficult to live on those lofty peaks day in and day out.

Jesus interrupted Peter's gallant defense in the garden, saving the situation and no doubt, Peter's life. In the blink of an eye He reached out and miraculously reattached the soldier's ear that Peter had lopped off.

Jesus intended that Peter live for Him, not die for Him. And He had one more master-to-student encounter planned in order to explain to him just what service He required.

After Christ's resurrection, He met the disciples at the lake for a good old fish breakfast. When they had finished eating, Jesus said to Peter, "Simon son of John, do you truly love me more than these?" (John 21:15) Some scholars believe, as I do, that because of the construction of the Greek language found here, Jesus wasn't asking, "Do you love me more than these other people." He was asking, "do you love me more than these other things." In that moment, he may have pointed to the boats and fishing nets laying near by. After all, it was Peter who told the rest of the disciples after Jesus' death that he was going back to fishing (John 21:3).

Jesus may have been saying, "Peter do you love me more than your previous life as a fisherman." Peter responded, "You know that I love you." That was the first spike of Peter's crucifixion. Jesus responded, "Feed my lambs." Once again Jesus said, "Simon son of John, do you truly love me?"

"Yes, Lord, you know that I love you," Peter answered back. That was spike number two. Then the third and final spike came in saying, "Simon, do you love me?" As the death of self was made complete, Peter cried out the word that a true crucified disciple finds on his lips, "Lord, you know all things; you know that I love you." Jesus fired back, "Feed my sheep."

Peter had received three spikes as hard as any Roman nails and probably just as painful. He understood that his immediate call was to service not to the martyr's altar.

There was a day coming in his old age when Peter would face that sudden moment of ultimate devotion. Jesus warned him of it, but for now Jesus had planned for Peter a much more difficult demonstration of his love. He wanted Peter to live for Him in obedience by feeding His sheep.

I have found that if you ask a room full of Christians this the-oretical question most will raise their hands, "If Christ asked you to die for Him, would you?" Yet I've found that if you ask, "Would you be willing to live anywhere God calls under any kind of con-dition?" fewer say yes. Fewer still said yes when asked, "Are you living for Him today."

The noble ox was ready to serve either on the altar or in the fields. Peter, after some struggle, became ready for either as well.

Unfortunately, there are far too many today who claim to be servants of Christ but who would have to admit that when it really gets down to it, they are ready for neither.

JUST DO IT

ASK YOURSELF, would you be willing to serve Christ in another country? Should this blank be filled with your name? _____, Do you love me? Feed my sheep. Maybe it's time to request some literature from your church on missions that they currently sup-port.

47
THY WILL BE DONE

*"Our Father in heaven, hallowed be your name,
your kingdom come, your will be done on earth as it is
in heaven."*

MATTHEW 6:9–10

JESUS KNEELED ALONE IN THE GARDEN of Gethsemane while his friends slept. He knew what was around the corner: torture and death. But something more horrible awaited. Jesus faced the prospect that He would soon be separated from His Father. Sweating blood, He cried out, "Father, if it is possible, let this cup pass from me, but nevertheless not my will be done but thy will." Jesus prayed the *sine qua non* of Christianity, "Thy will be done, not mine."

Some find this painful vignette in the life of Jesus tough to read. They understand the true agony of surrendering your will to God. Still others find it difficult to believe God too "nice" to directly "will" a crucifixion. After all, isn't His primary duty to ensure the happiness of His unique creation by granting them the "desires of their hearts"? In this belief system, God is reduced to a cosmic genie that comes out of the bottle when we pray in order to make our dreams come true.

Is it really God's job to make our dreams come true?

Yes, but only when we begin to dream His dreams. When we dream of holiness, we will become holy. When we plead for courage, we will be granted bravery. When we long to love others, we will be given the chance to show it.

God will not be reduced to an omnipotent Santa Claus that Christians pray to in order to get their wish lists filled. The object of our prayer is to discover *His* wish list and prepare our hearts to do it. "The name it and claim it" movement has in many cases overlooked this. As a result, the movement has degenerated into a repugnant distortion of the biblical doctrines of prayer, faith, and service. Paul teaches that only "men of corrupt mind, who have been robbed of the truth . . . think that godliness is a means to financial gain" (1 Timothy 6:5). In fact, godliness often directly contributes to material poverty. Success in the kingdom of God means that the damaged moral image of God is being restored to its pre-Eden beauty. It means to become holy as He is holy. Those who hunger and thirst after righteousness will receive the most valuable reward of all: to see God and live in His presence. If this is your wish list, it will be abundantly granted because it was Christ's wish list from the beginning.

Joshua had dreamed all his life of rising in the military to the rank of commander. When it finally was thrust upon him, it wasn't what he expected. Moses put him in charge and commanded him to be courageous, but that was easier said than done. As Joshua gazed across the plain to the walled city of Jericho, doubt and fear gripped him. These were the same men that spies had once said, "We are but grasshoppers in their sight." The walls of Jericho were so thick that, even at the top, two chariots could ride abreast. Joshua wondered how he would conquer this impregnable fortress. Then the answer came. A man suddenly stood before him with a drawn sword. Joshua asked, "'Are you for us or for our enemies?' 'Neither,' he replied, 'but as commander of the army of the LORD I have now come'" (Joshua 5:13–14).

Did you hear what he didn't say? He didn't say he had come to join Joshua's fight. He didn't say he had come to the rescue. He said he'd come to take over. He had no intention of being a comrade. He came to be the commander.

Jesus is not interested in joining our battles. He is not our partner. He is not an associate. He is our God. His kingdom is not a democracy. He's not impressed by our vain plans, nor are His plans voted on by us. He is our sovereign Lord and God. He doesn't take sides, He takes over. We do not serve at His side, we serve at His feet.

We mustn't pray for God to join our battles. We must follow Him into His battles. We mustn't ask Him to bless our plans. We must pray to be led where He is blessing. We mustn't ask Him to do our will. We should ask Him to reveal His will and empower us to do it. It is His will that is being established on Earth "as it is in heaven."

Do you wish to always succeed and never fail? Then never fail to seek His will. The will of God is unstoppable. If Jesus leads us up to our great walls of Jericho, they will fall if we march at His command. While He calls us to conquer unimaginable enemies, we will not be crushed when we pray "thy will, not mine be done."

JUST DO IT

PRAYFULLY FILL IN these blanks:

God wants me to be more _____.

God wants me to do more _____.

God wants me to want more _____.

God wants me to want less _____.

48
SAY WHAT?

"I form the light and create darkness, I bring prosperity and create disaster; I, the LORD, do all these things."
ISAIAH 45:7

IN BIBLE COLLEGE, MY SPEECH TEACHER told us this simple formula for getting your message across. He said, "First, tell them what you're going to tell them, then tell 'em, then tell 'em what you just told them." Here's where I tell you what I've been telling you throughout this entire book.

Worry, unguided emotions, and inactivity are three powerful enemies to spiritual life. Any one of the three can be a deadly poison. Thankfully, God has given us an antidote for each.

The *sovereignty of God* teaches us not to worry but to go forward in His strength with the certainty that the same God who holds the world together by the word of His power can hold your future together as well. The *Scripture* is our only reliable moral light for decision-making. It illuminates our path through the dense fog of human emotion or desire. And it is always, always, always trustworthy. Finally, *service* is the way that we demonstrate to God, the world, and to ourselves that Jesus is truly Lord. It is only by taking those tiny steps of service that the next step on our path becomes visible.

SOVEREIGNTY

MOSES SENT spies into the forbidden land of the "ites" (Amalekites, Hittites, Canaanites, etc.). All but Caleb came back reporting that it would be impossible to conquer this land filled with giants. "We saw the Nephilim there," they said. And as a result the children of Israel "seemed like grasshoppers" in their own eyes (Numbers 13:33).

Caleb, on the other hand, looked at the land from a different point of view. He saw a land that flowed with milk and honey. He focused his attention, not on the adversaries, but on the opportunities. While others looked up at the problem through the eyes of grasshoppers, Caleb looked down at the land God had promised from the hilltop of divine view point. His conclusion was, "We should go up and take possession of the land, *for we can certainly do it*" (Numbers 13:30, emphasis added).

Contemporary Christian music performer Steve Wiggins wrote in his song "Jesus Is Your Friend":

> *Take the biggest thing that's got you down.*
> *Stand it up right next to God.*
> *Anyone can see who's bigger now.*
> *It doesn't take no astronaut.*

It doesn't take an astronaut to know that all problems pale in comparison to His strength. If you are on the Lord's side, victory is certain. When Caleb said, "We can," it was because he understood the sovereign God of the universe guaranteed the victory.

SCRIPTURE

PAUL WAS physically forced out of the ancient city of Thessalonica. After preaching the Word of God in the synagogue, a group of zealous members of the Jewish faith recruited some thugs and stirred up a riot. Dodging the violence, Paul and his pals simply continued on to the city of Berea. But Paul's opposition didn't give up that easily. Though it meant walking nearly seventy-five miles, they followed Paul to Berea dead set on shutting the apostle up. These weren't people who just hated Paul and had some time on their hands. These were deeply religious people who resented Paul calling Jesus the Messiah. They were convinced that Christ's crucifixion was solid evidence that He could not have been the promised one. Consequently, they were sincerely willing to demonstrate their piety through personal sacrifice, not realizing that they had become a perfect example of ignorance on fire.

In contrast, the believers in Berea were said to be "of more noble character than the Thessalonians, for they received the message with great eagerness and examined the Scriptures every day to see if what Paul said was true" (Acts 17:11). God considered them to have more depth and virtue. They didn't walk seventy-five miles to heckle those they believed to be heretics. They simply examined Paul's testimony in light of the teachings of the Bible.

Passion is not an acceptable substitute for being right. In fact, passion can sometimes steer us off the right path. God's Word is not subject to every change in the cultural or moral wind. It alone is reliable to lead us into God's eternal will.

SERVICE

NOAH BUILT the ark and it wasn't even raining . . . yet! In fact, it had probably never rained on earth before. Genesis 2:6 tells us that before the great flood "streams came up from the earth and watered the whole surface of the ground." Many Christian scientists believe that the predeluvian world was surrounded by a giant canopy of water. The effect was that the earth was like a huge greenhouse. No rain had ever fallen from the sky. Plants were watered each evening by what the King James Version of the Bible calls a "mist" (Genesis 2:5). So you can imagine how it sounded when God commanded Noah to build a boat the size of an aircraft carrier in his front yard. Furthermore, just think about the ridicule from the neighbors as year after year Noah and his sons spent all their available time and money building a boat to protect them from water that was suppose to fall from the sky. Preposterous right? Not to Noah. God said, "Make yourself an ark" (Genesis 6:14) and "Noah *did* . . . just as God commanded."

A parked car is unsteerable. If we are going to discover the next leg of the journey we will discover it while on the move. Just go, and God will lead.

JUST DO IT

DON'T BE overwhelmed by all the areas of your Christian life that may need serious attention. Ask the Lord to help pick one problem at a time to deal with. The victory is won one tiny step at a time. May God bless you!

TOPICAL INDEX

SERVICE

Scripture Index

2 Corinthians 11:14 (chap. 6)
James 3:7–8 (chap. 7)
1 John 1:8–9 (chap. 8)
Hebrews 4:15 (chap. 14)
Romans 12:1 (chap. 15)
1 John 2:3 (chap. 18)
1 Corinthians 12:7 (chap. 20)
1 Corinthians 14:12 (chap. 20)
1 Peter 2:12 (chap. 21)
Hebrews 10:25 (chap. 25)
Ephesians 4:17 (chap. 30)
Galatians 5:17–24 (chap. 31)
Galatians 2:20 (chap. 36)
James 1:2–4 (chap. 40)